Real World

Colouring Book

For Advanced Users & Adults

50 Images

Created From Real Life Photos
For You To Colour As You Please.

ISBN 978-0-359-93582-6
90000
9 780359 935826

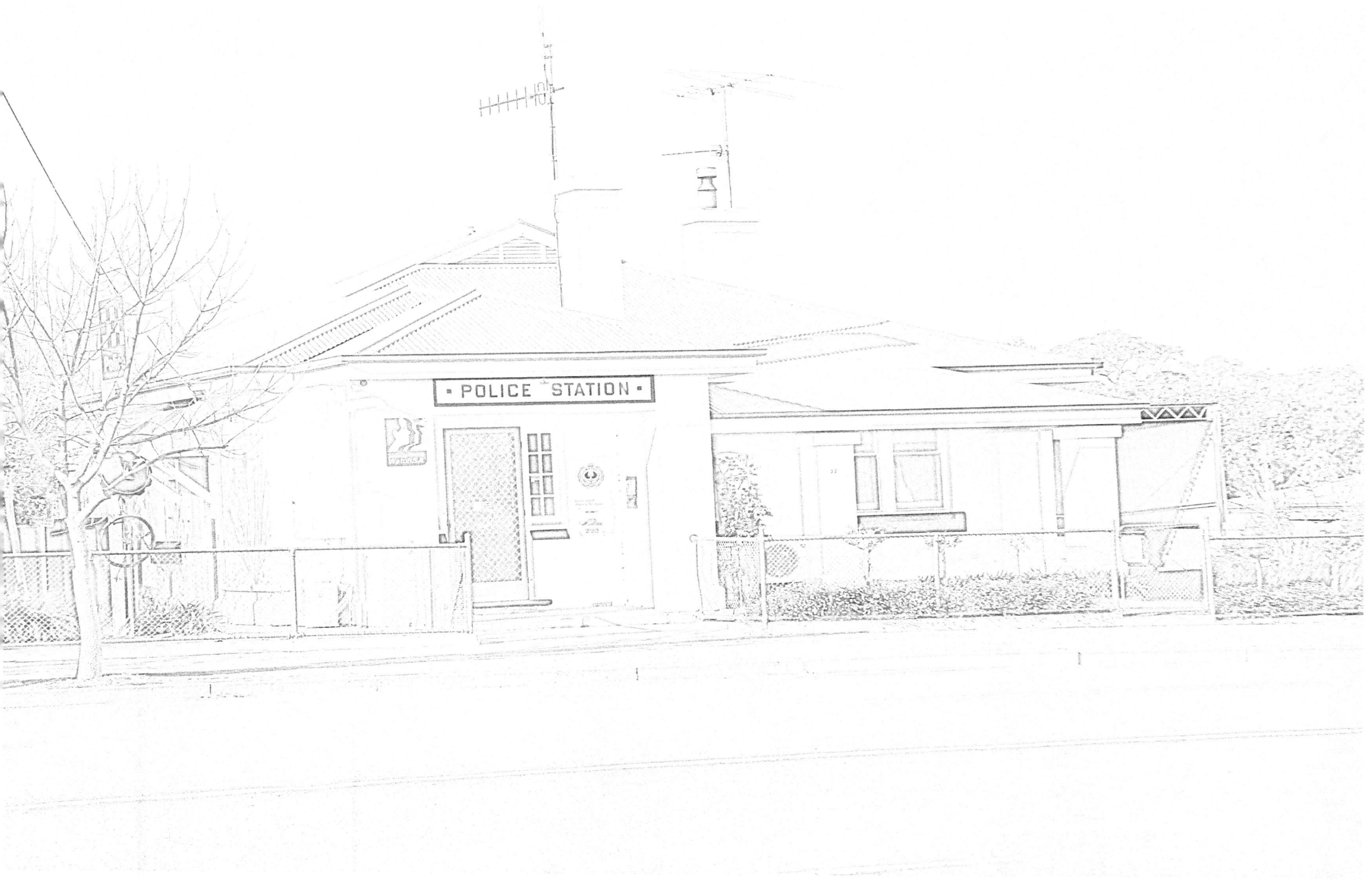
• POLICE STATION •

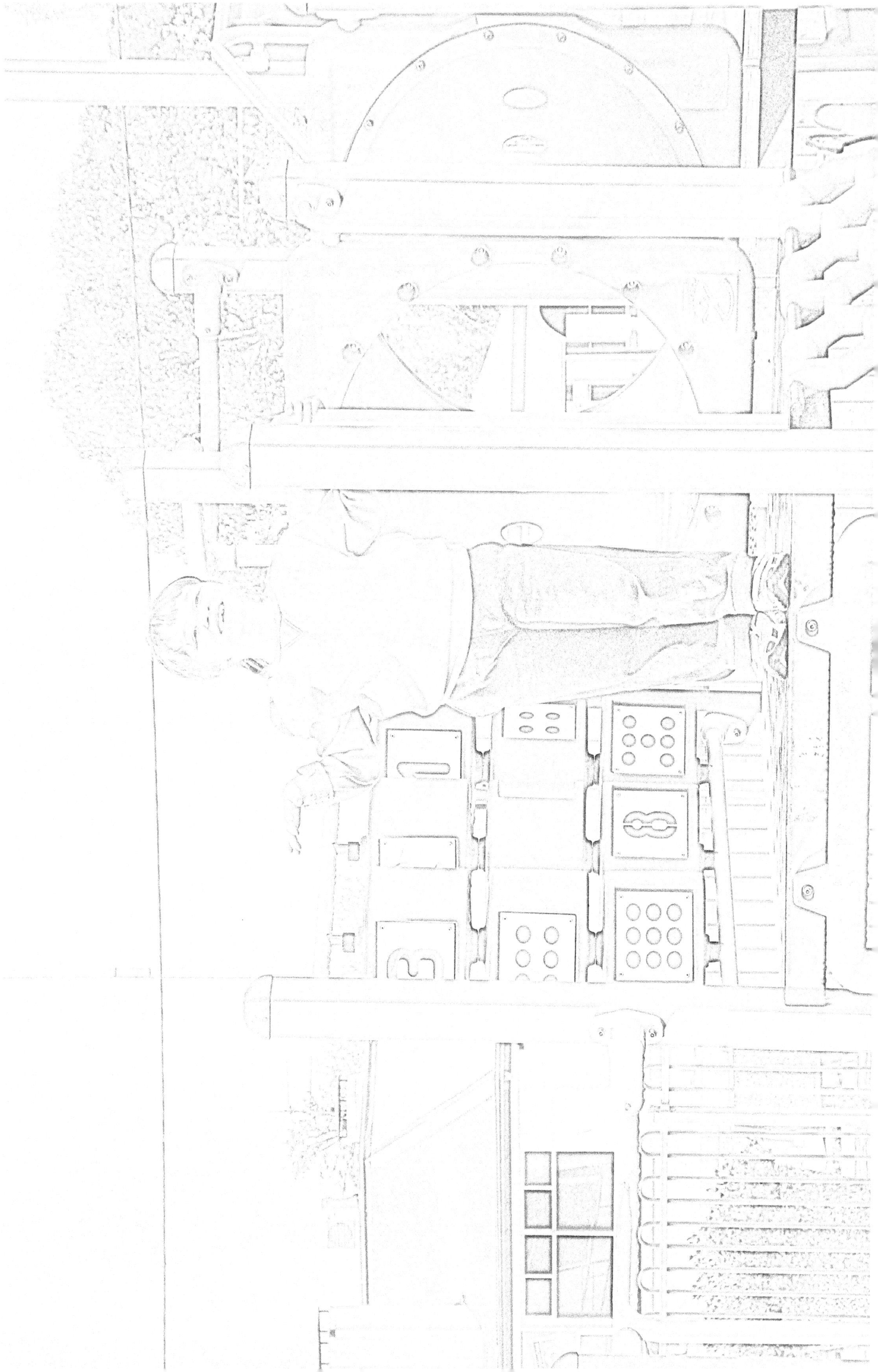

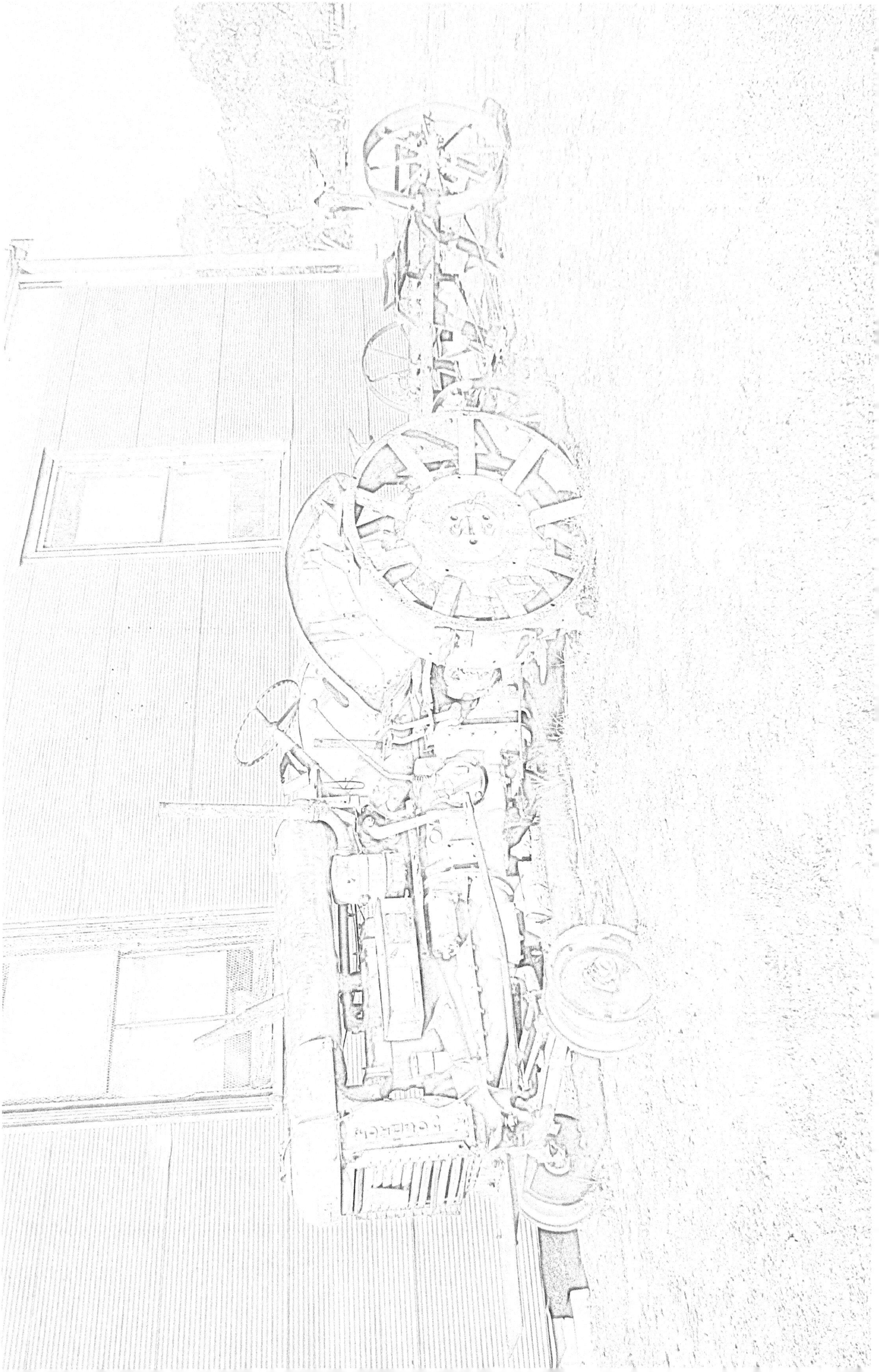

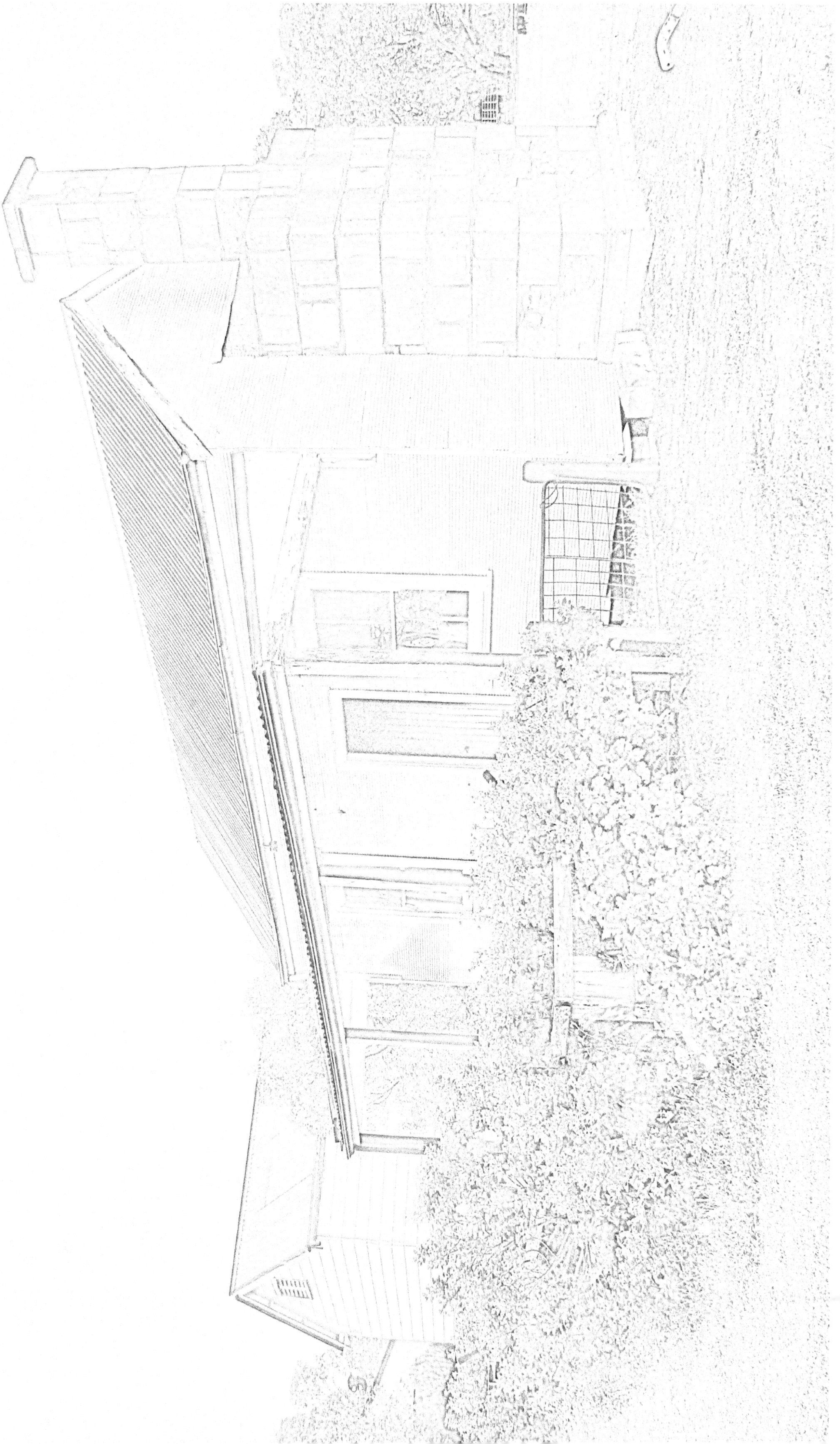

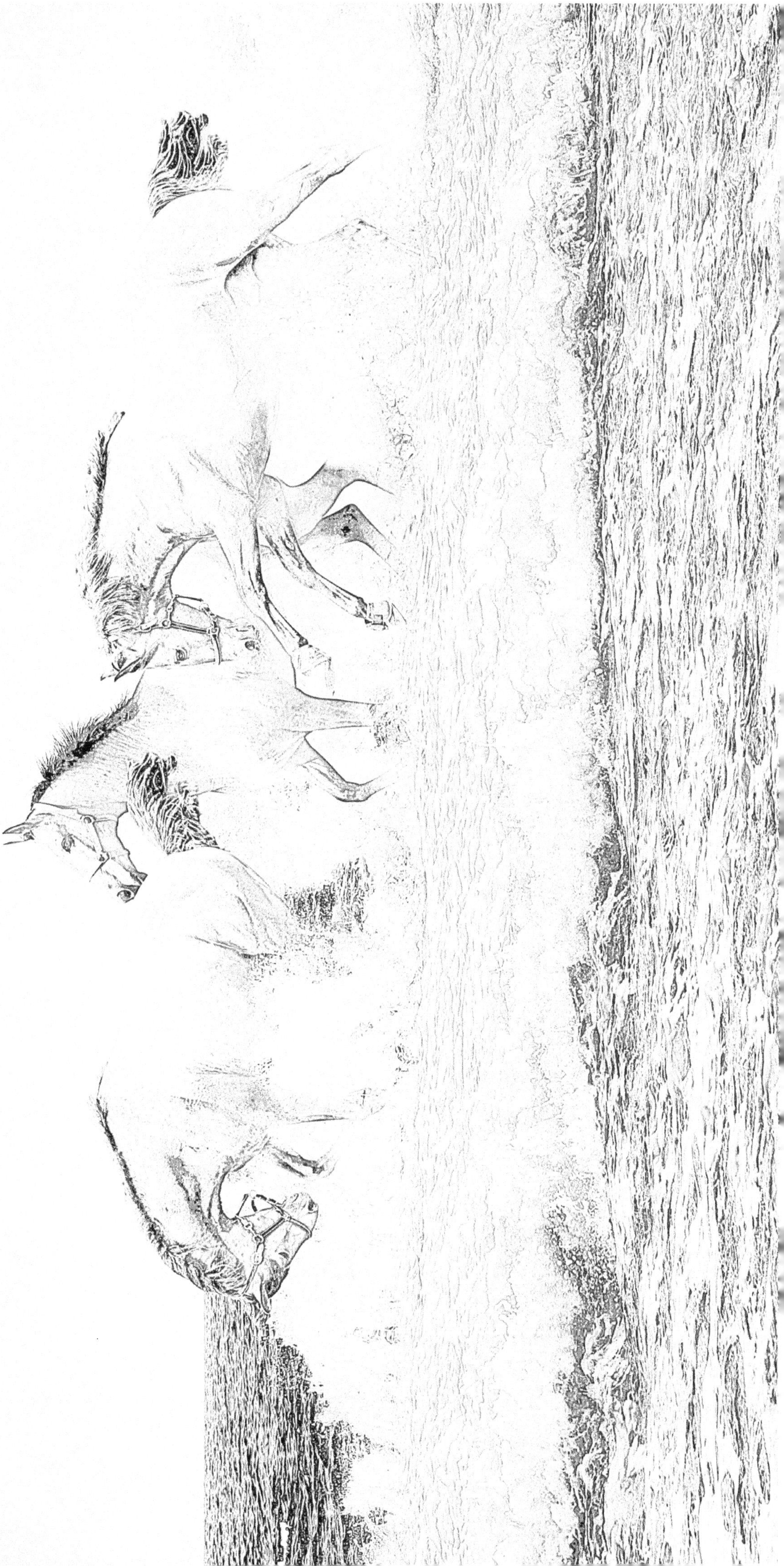

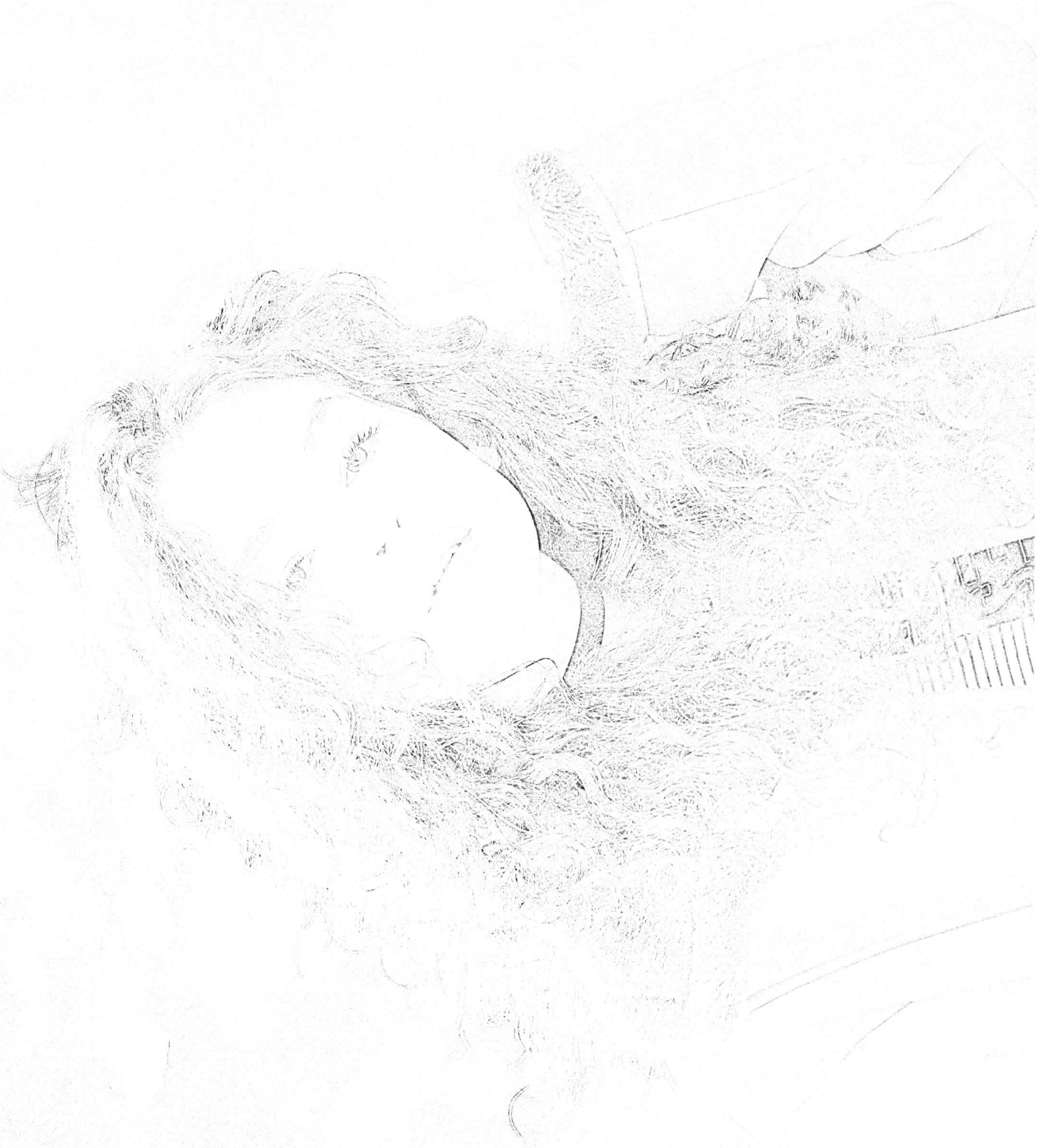

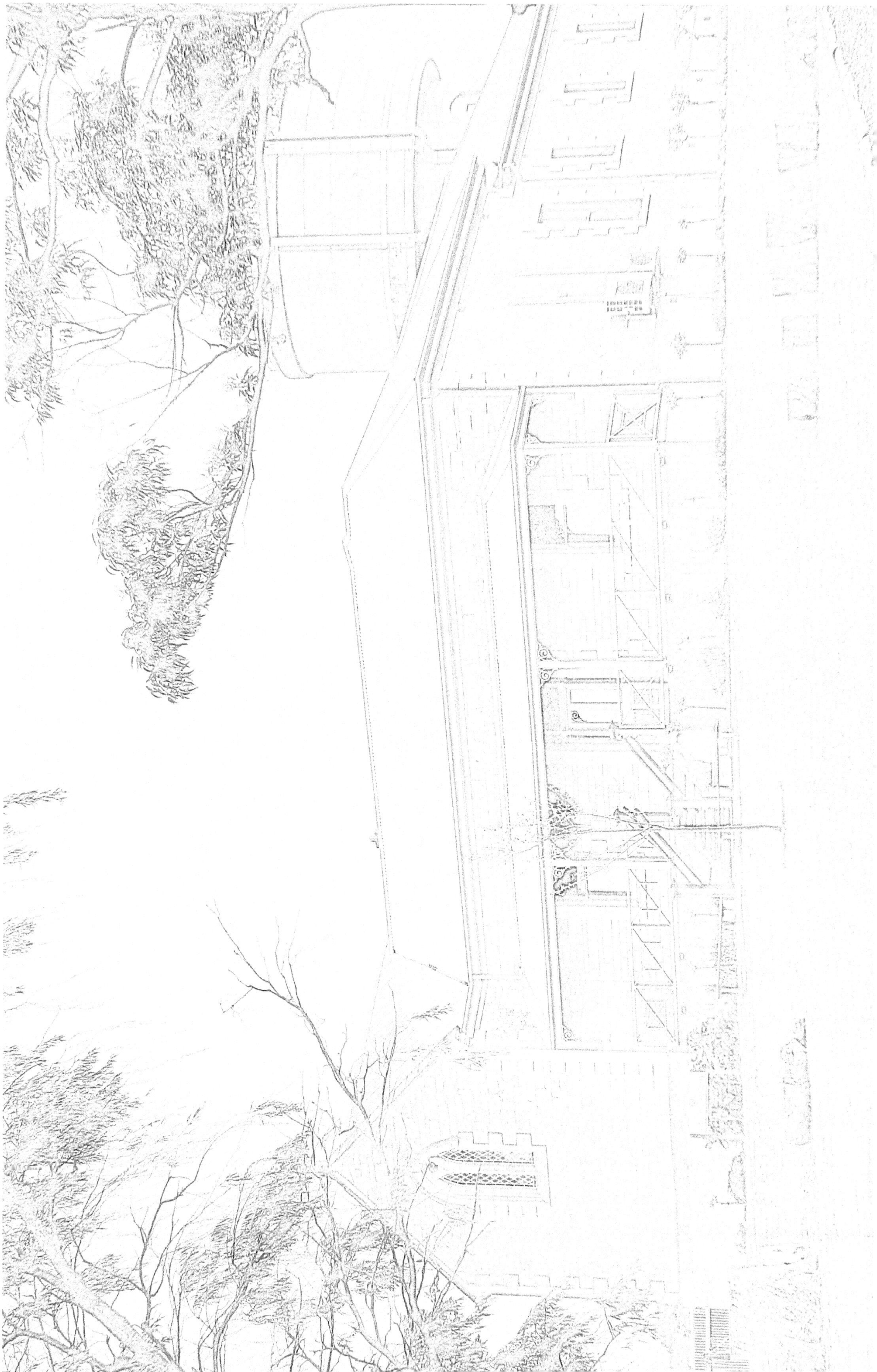

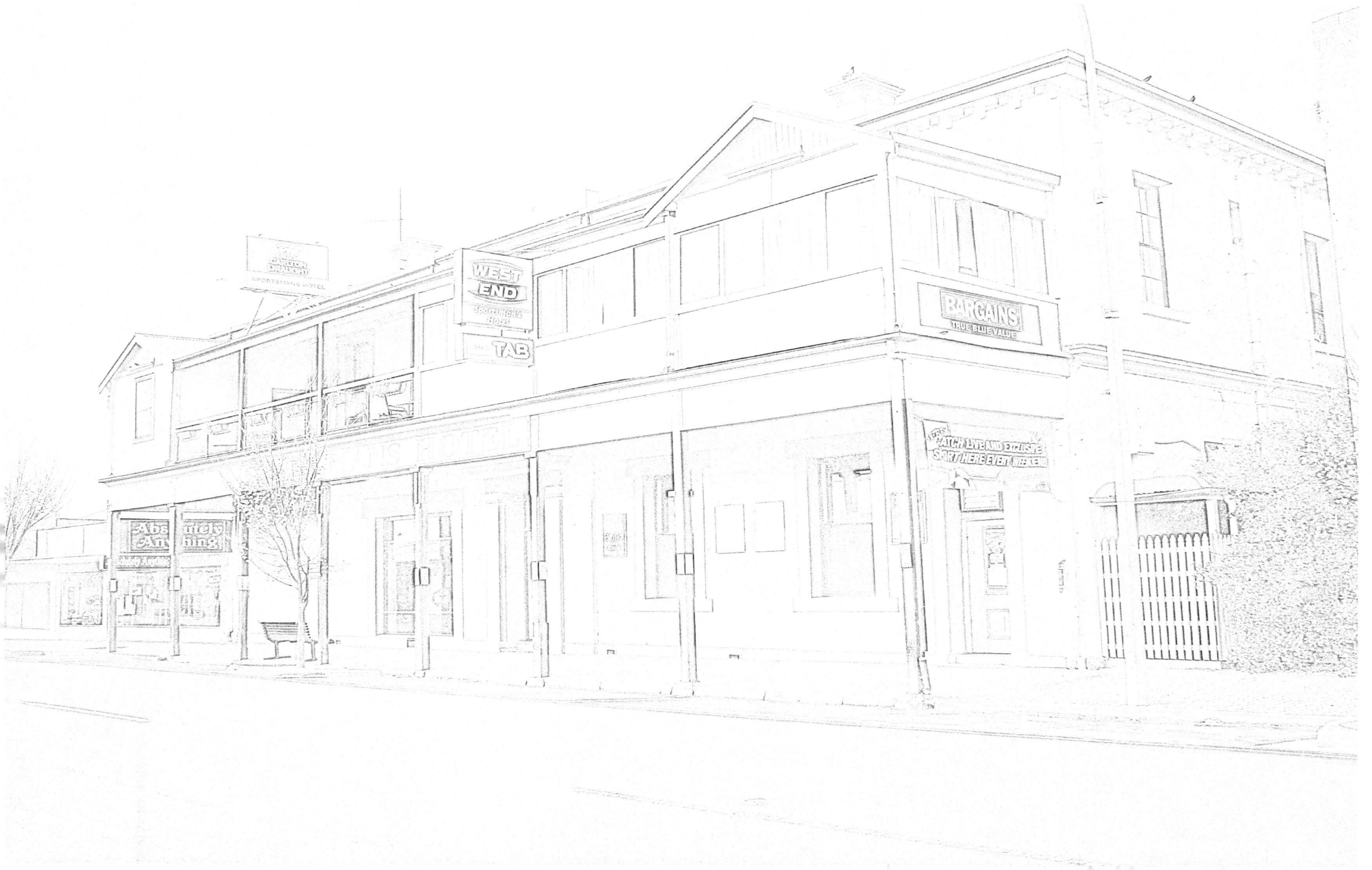
SPORTSMANS HOTEL
WEST END
TAB
BARGAINS
TRUE BLUE VALUE
WATCH LIVE AND EXCLUSIVE
SPORT HERE EVERY WEEKEND

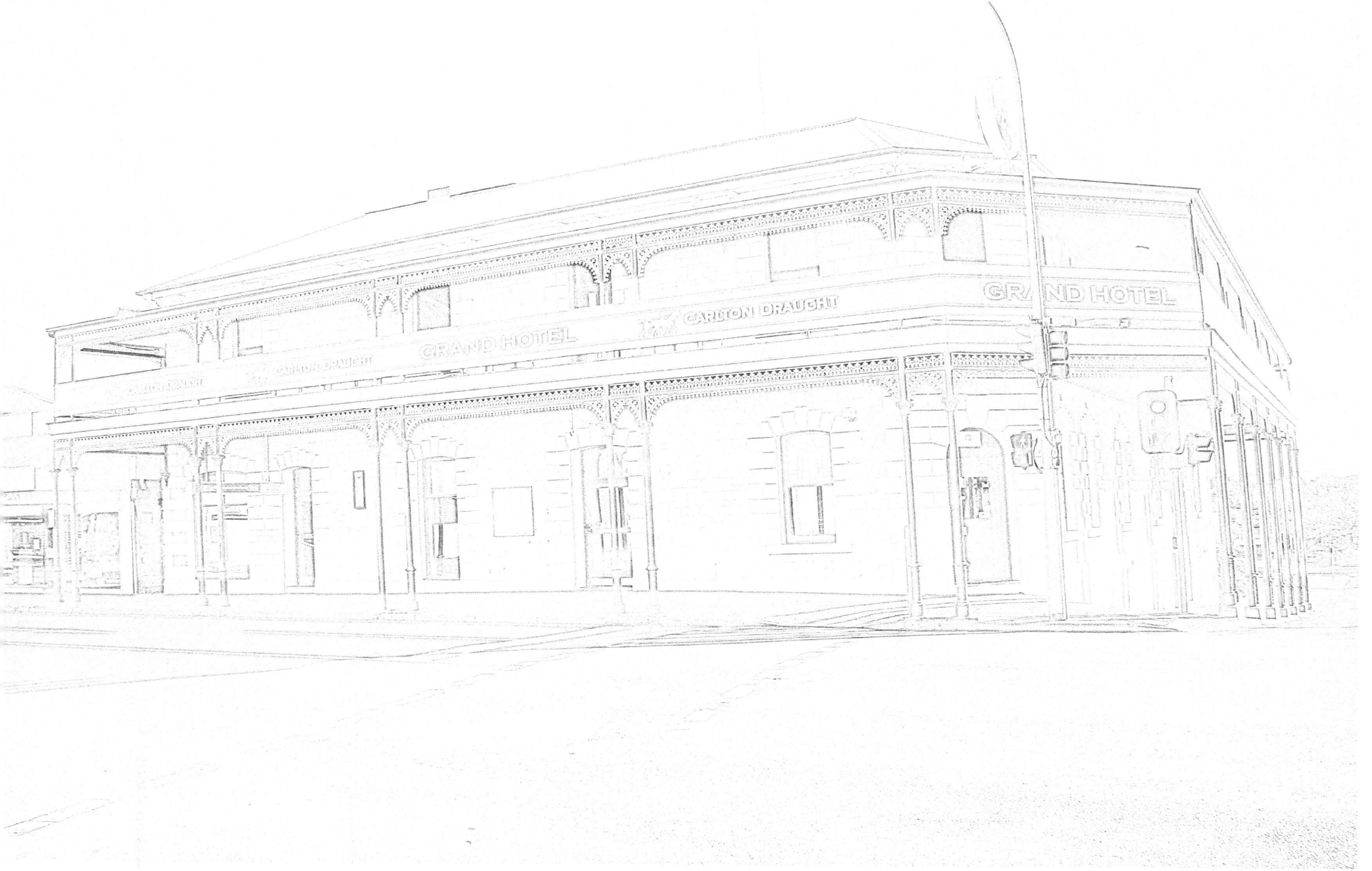
GRAND HOTEL
CARLTON DRAUGHT
GRAND HOTEL
CARLTON DRAUGHT

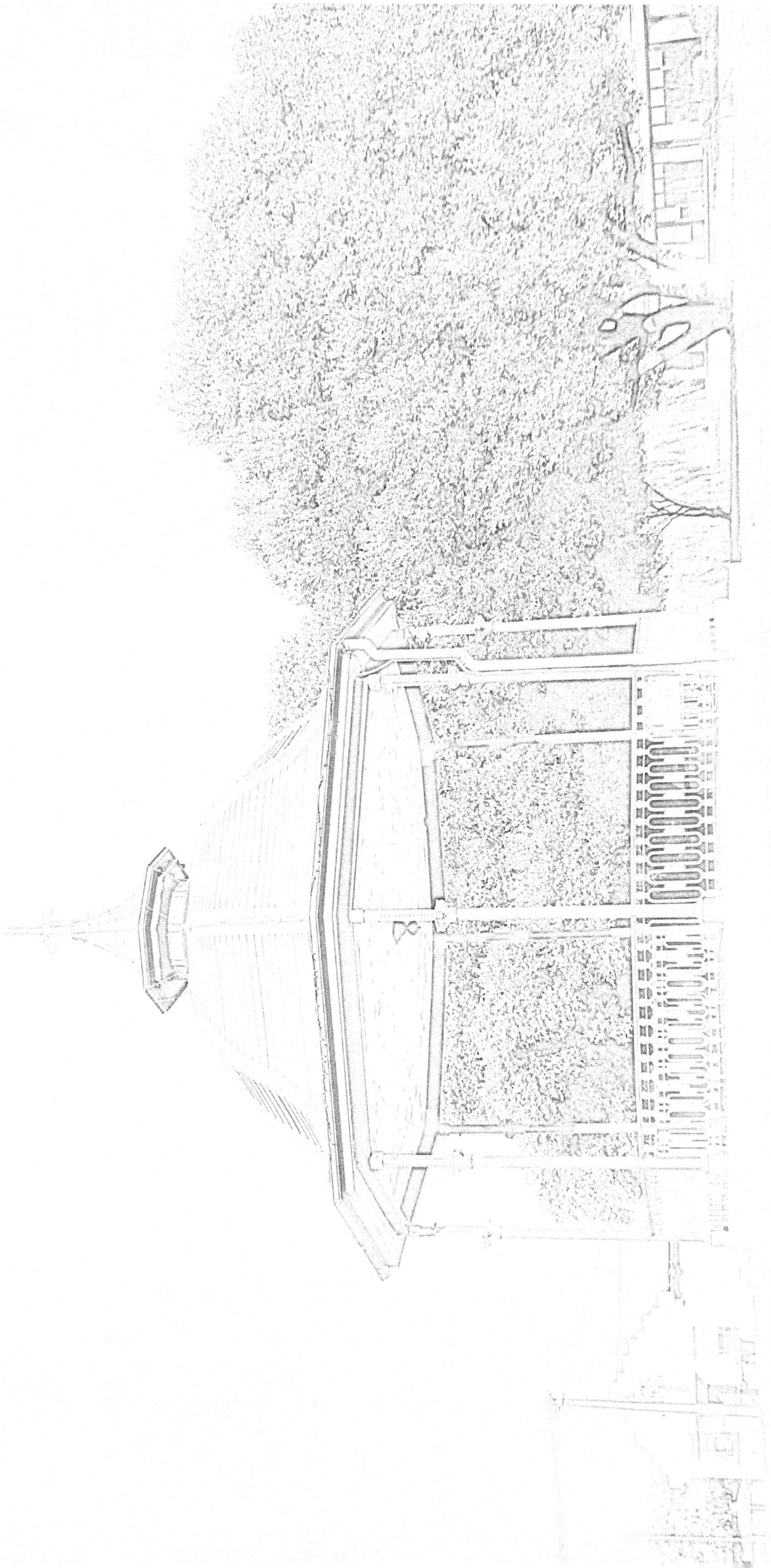

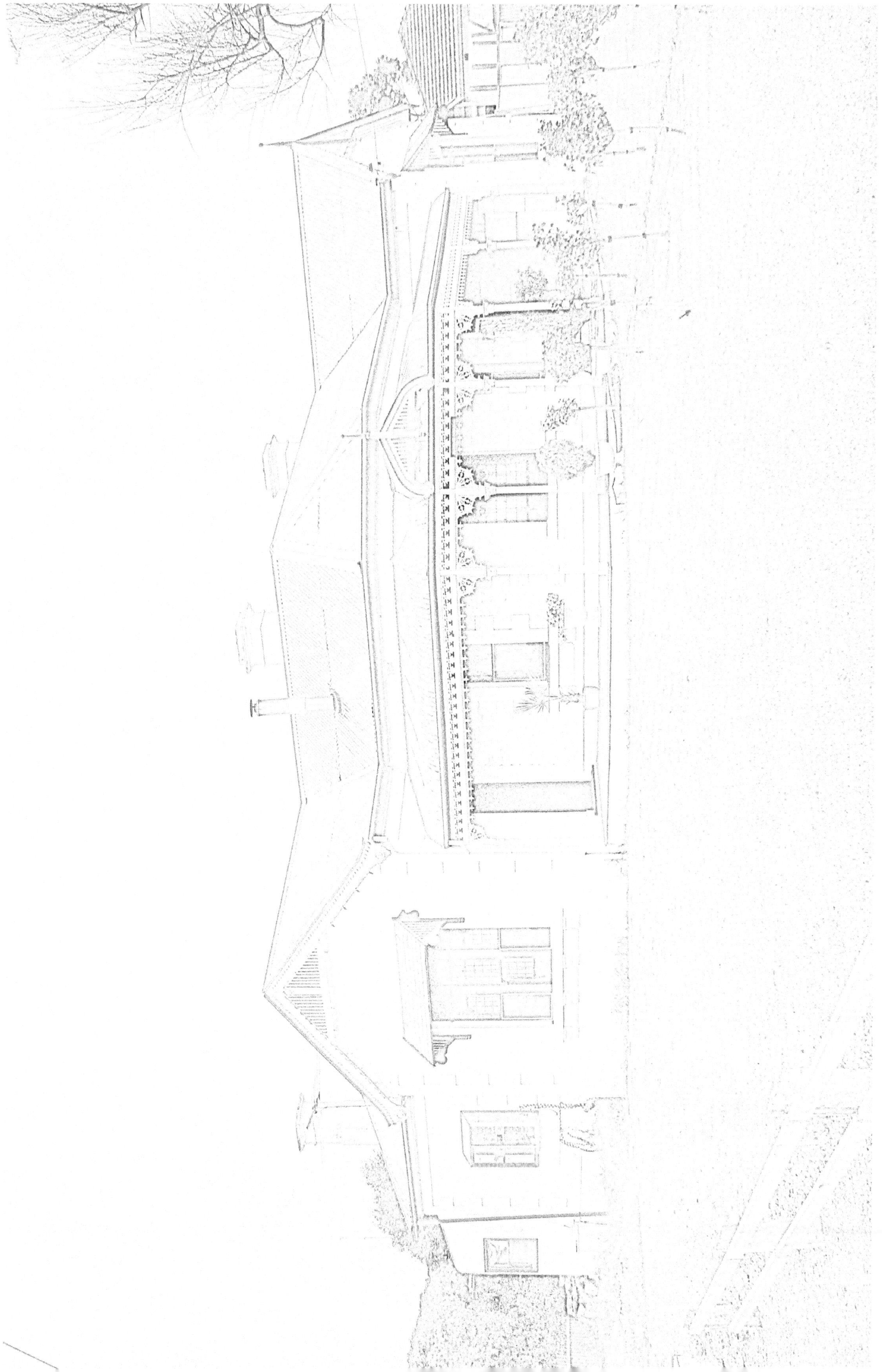

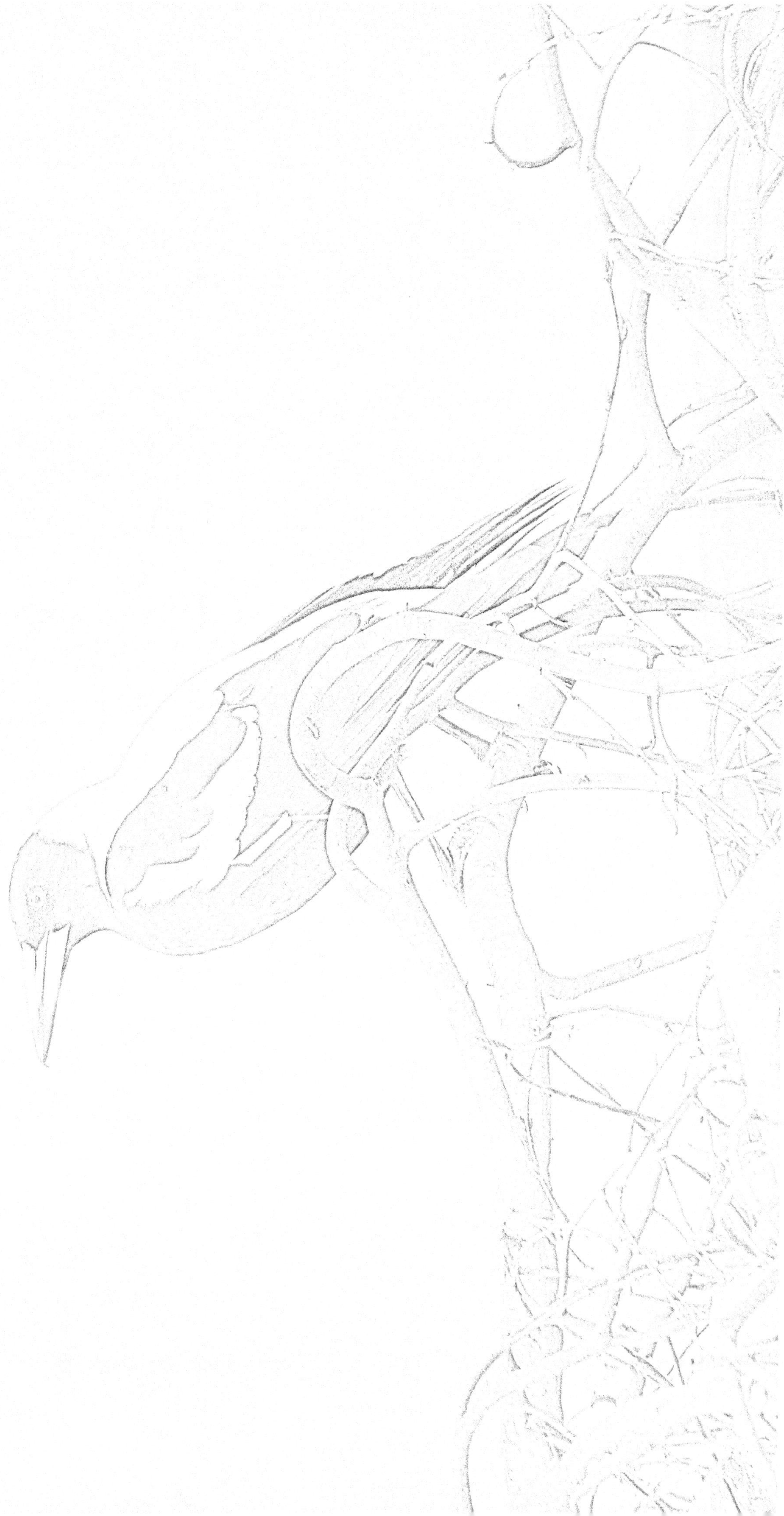

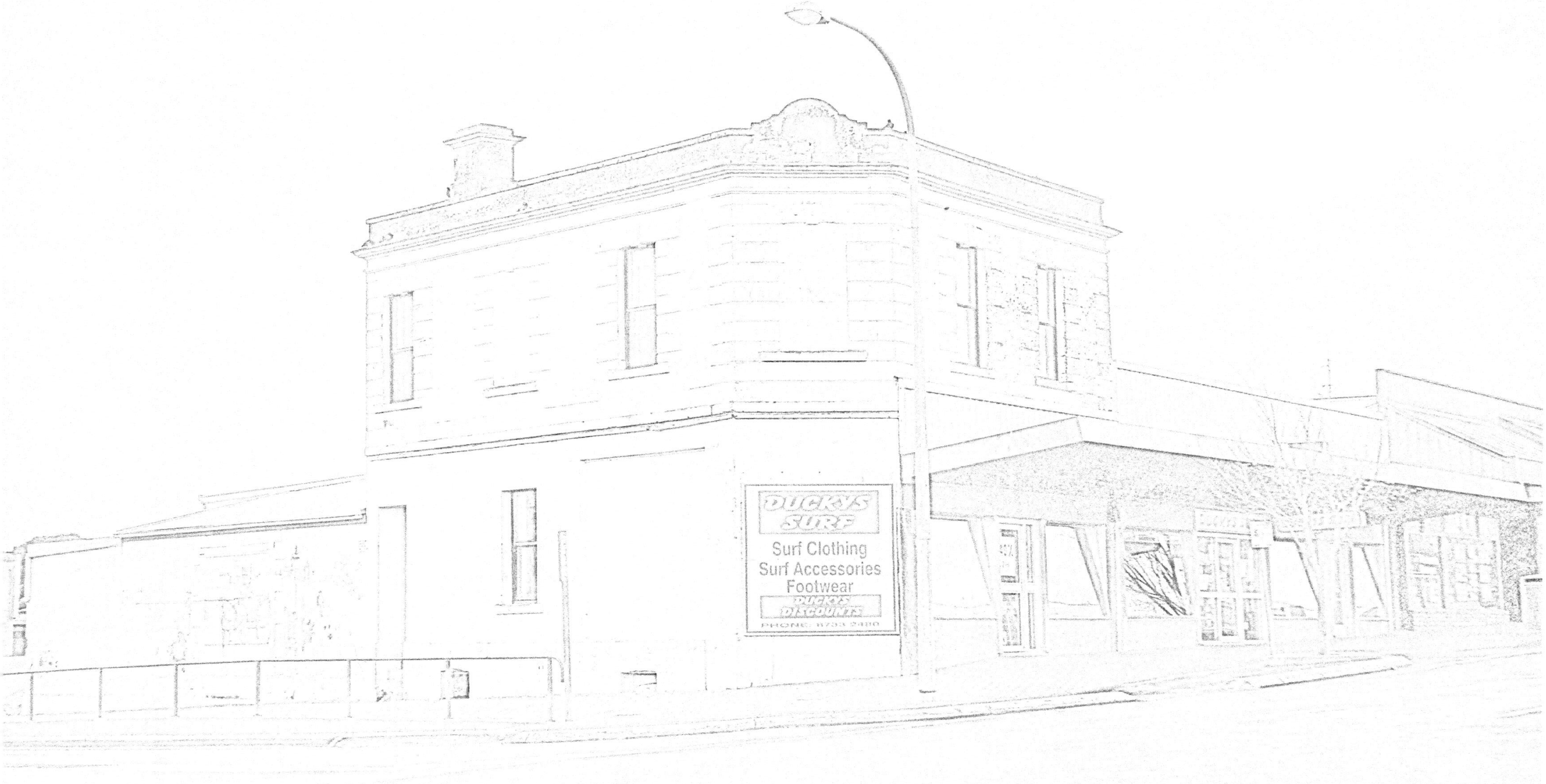
DUCKYS SURF
Surf Clothing
Surf Accessories
Footwear
DUCKYS DISCOUNTS

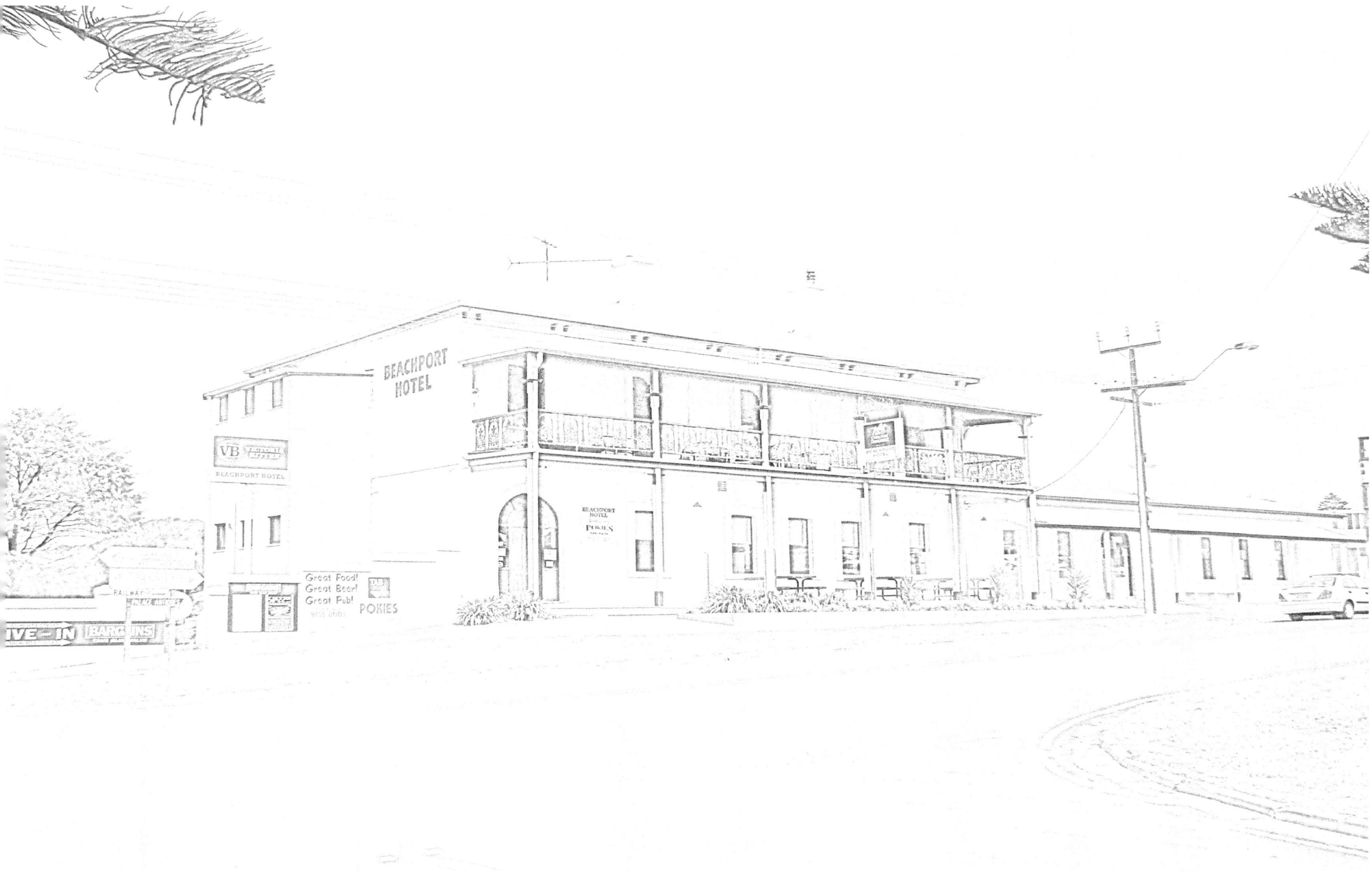
BEACHPORT HOTEL
VB
BEACHPORT HOTEL
Great Food!
Great Beer!
Great Pub!
POKIES
BEACHPORT HOTEL
POKIES
RAILWAY
IVE-IN
BARGAINS

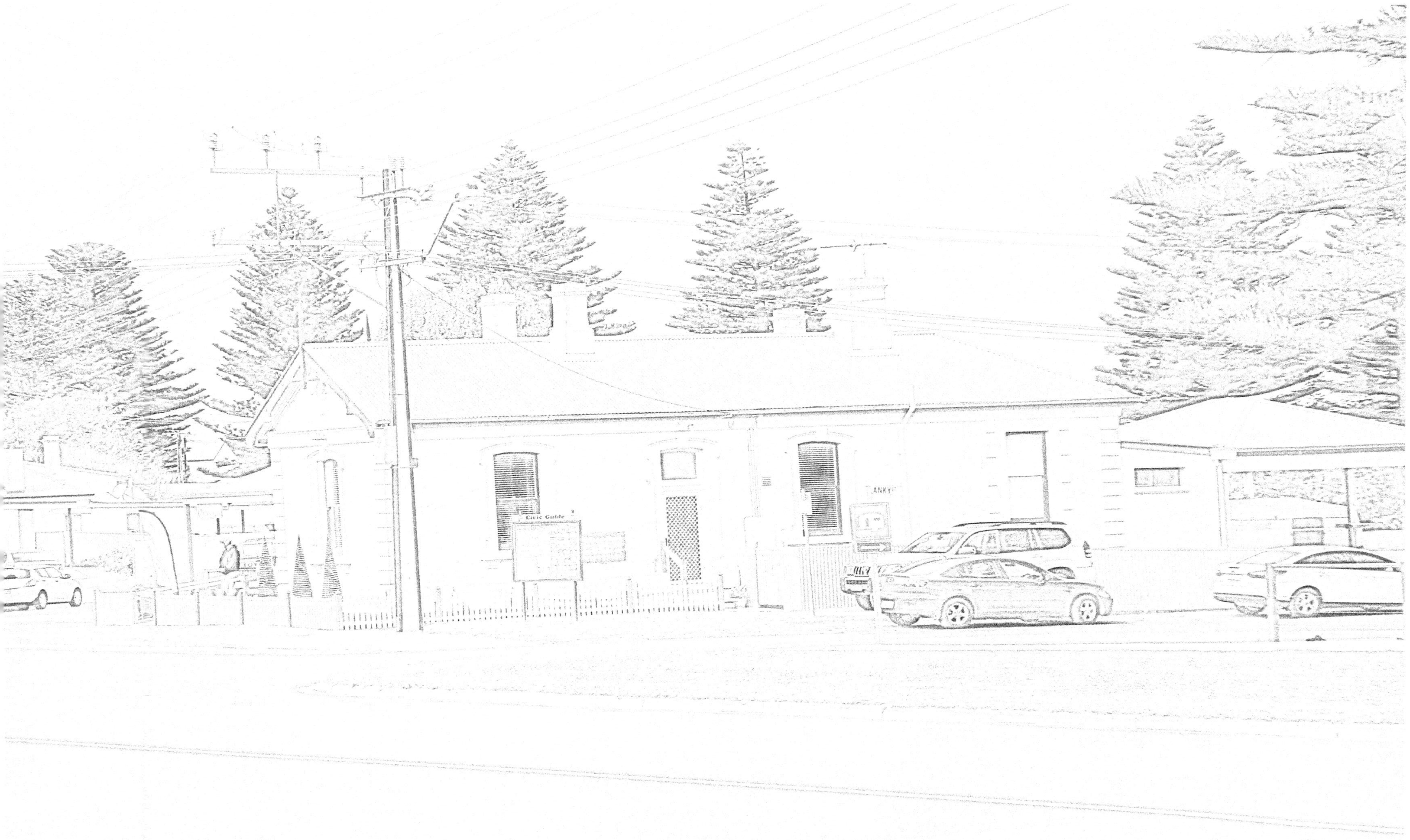
Civic Guide

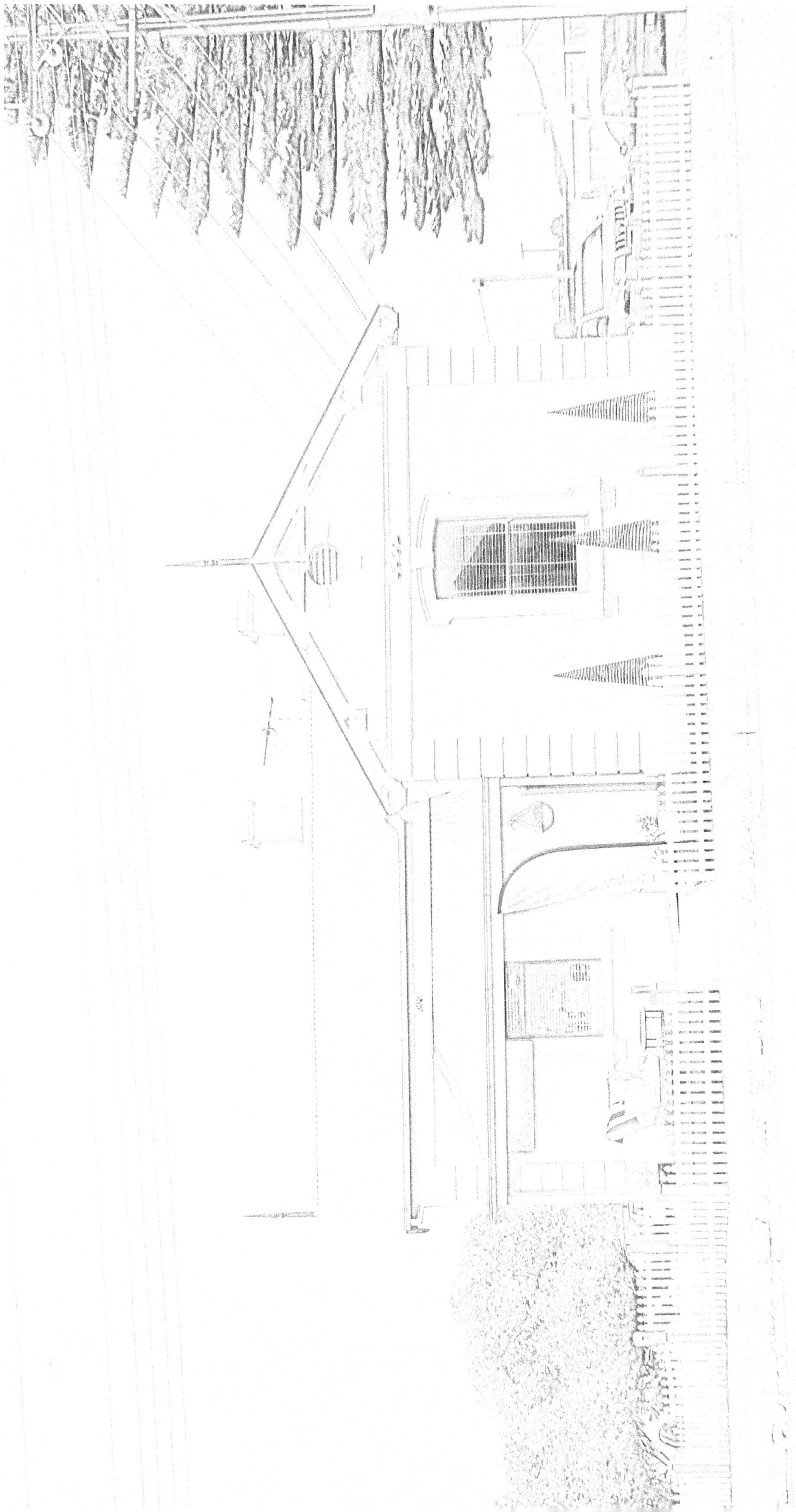

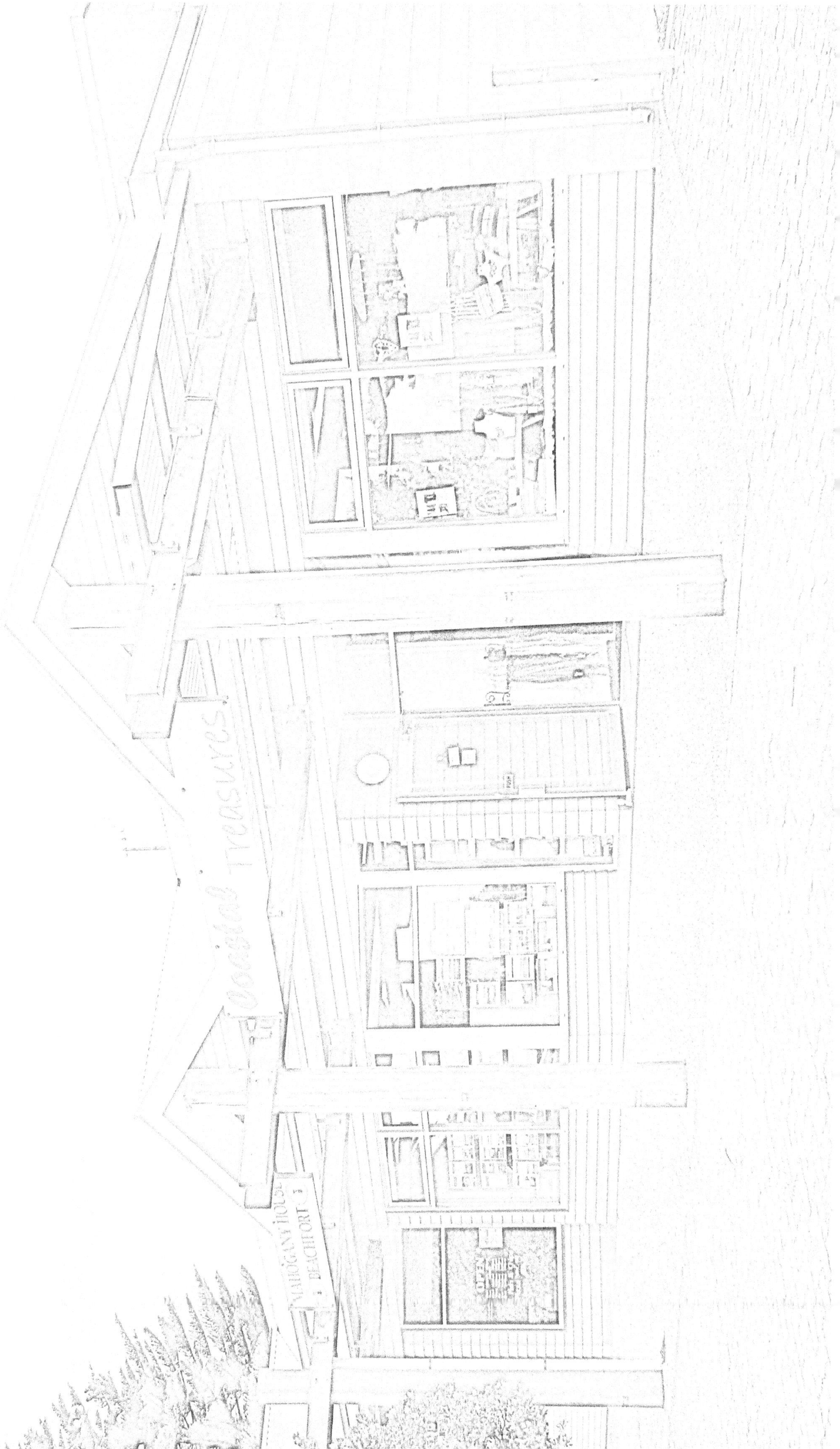
Coastal Treasures
MAHOGANY HOUSE
BEAUFORT

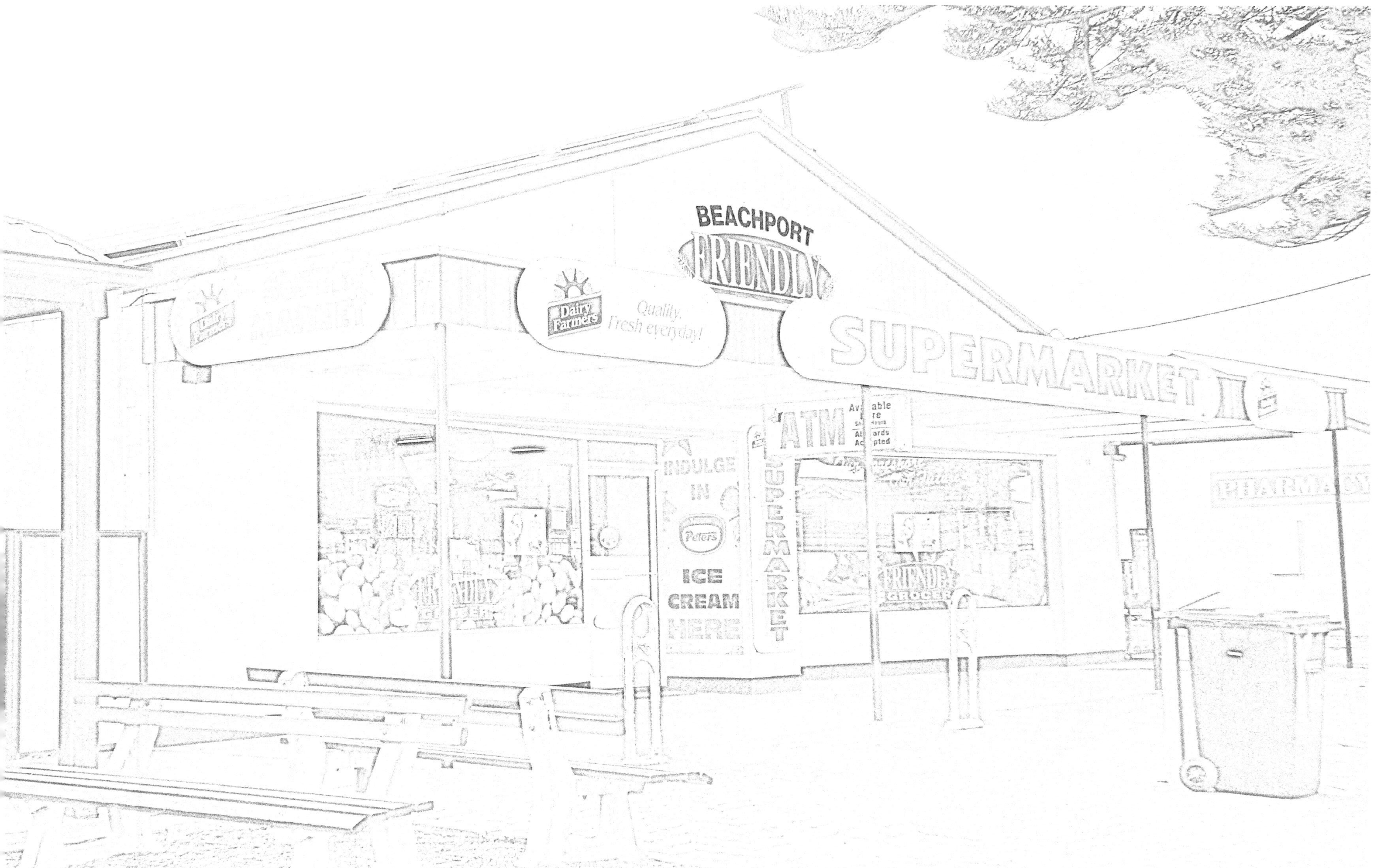
BEACHPORT
FRIENDLY
SUPERMARKET
Dairy Farmers
Quality, Fresh everyday!
ATM
INDULGE IN
Peters
ICE CREAM HERE
SUPERMARKET
PHARMACY

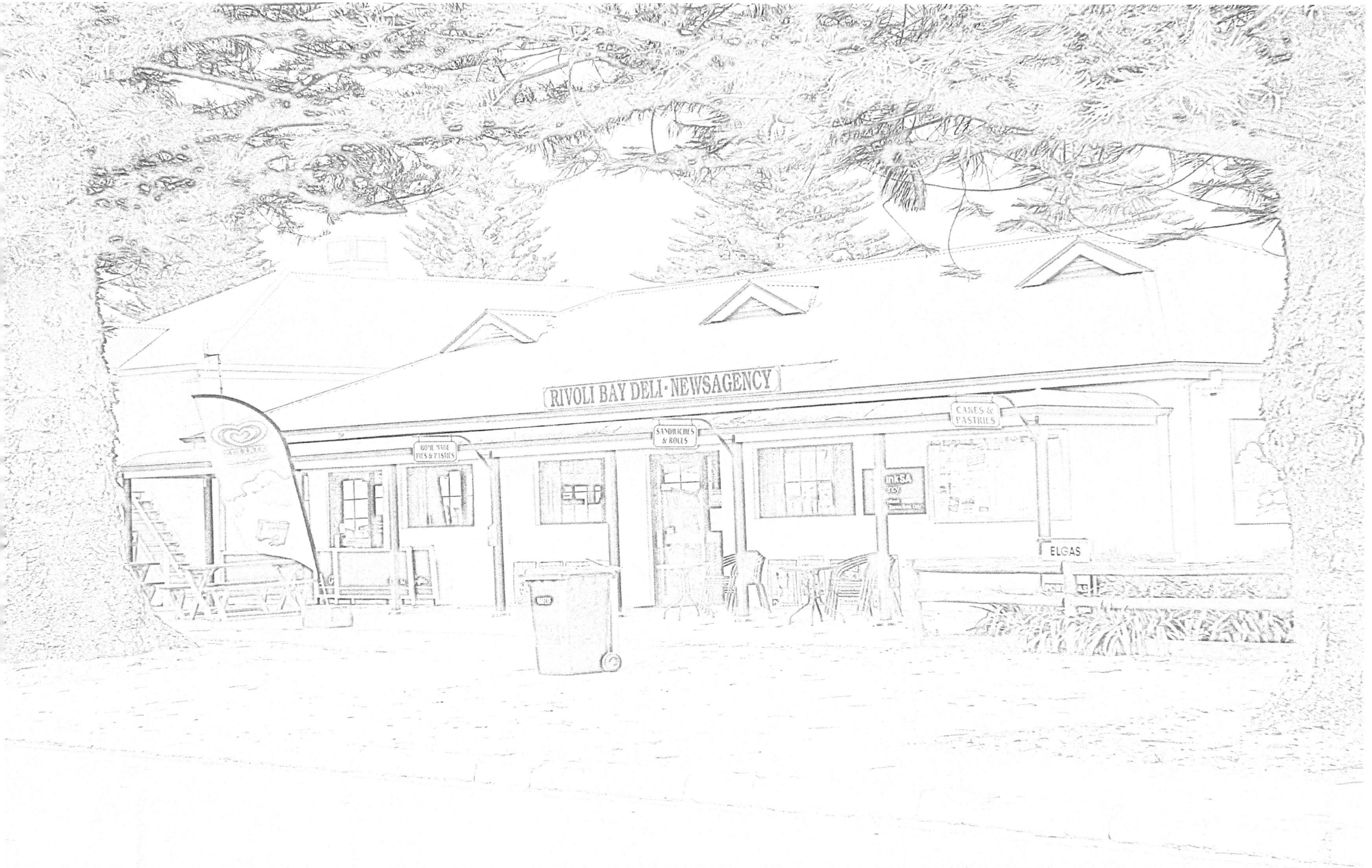
RIVOLI BAY DELI · NEWSAGENCY
HOME MADE PIES & PASTRIES
SANDWICHES & ROLLS
CAKES & PASTRIES
ELGAS

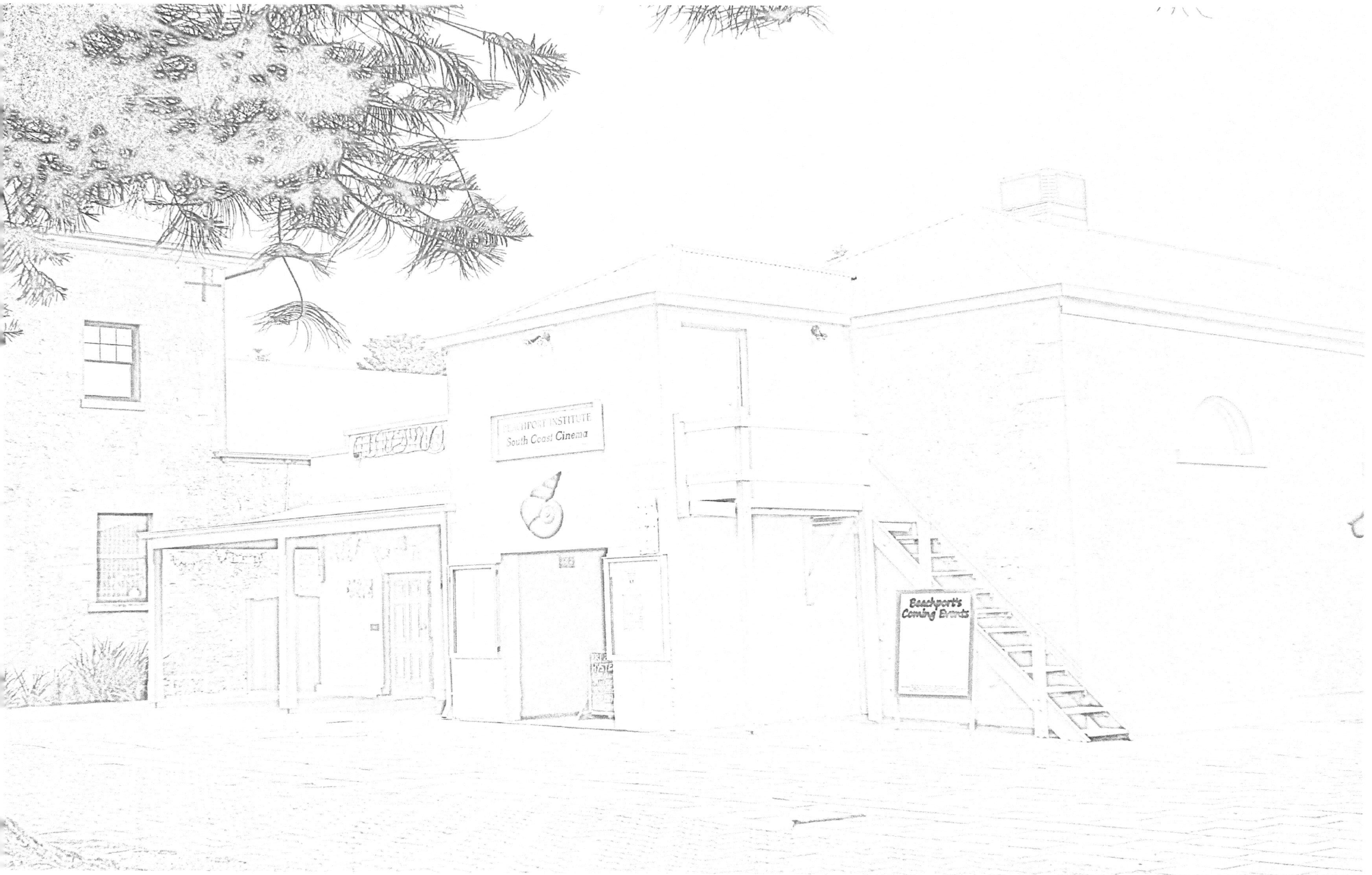
South Coast Cinema
Beachport's
Coming Events

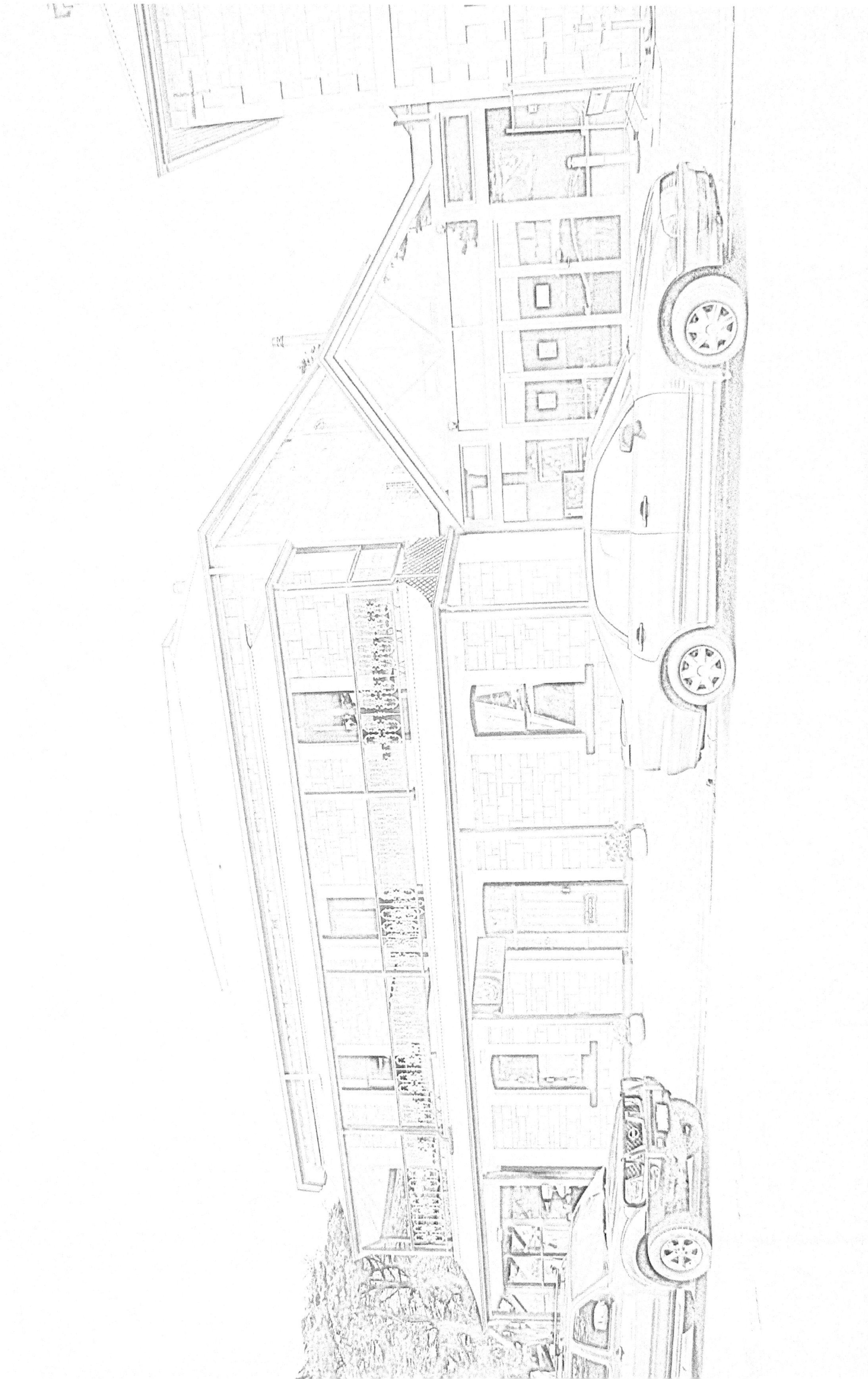

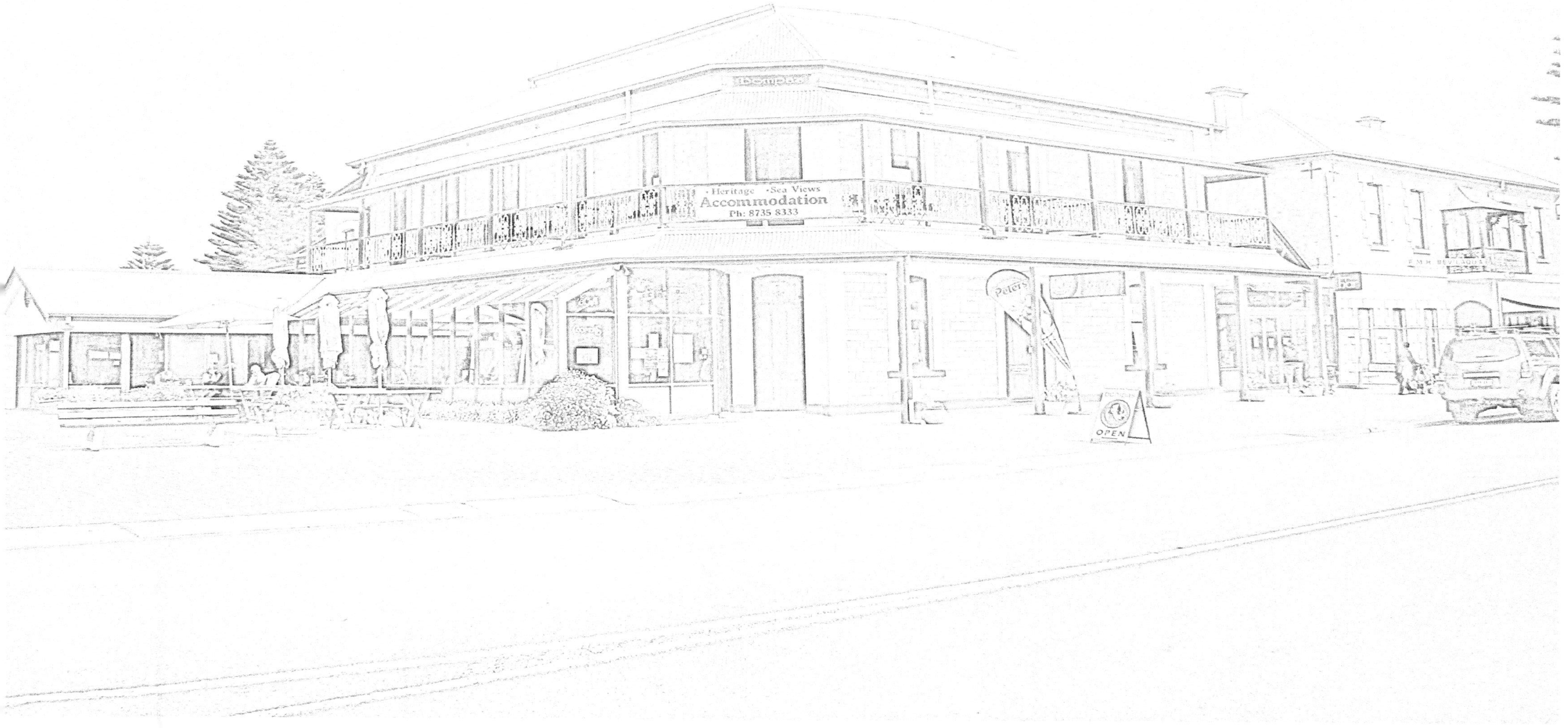

• Heritage • Sea Views
Accommodation
Ph: 8735 8333
Peters
OPEN

LANKY

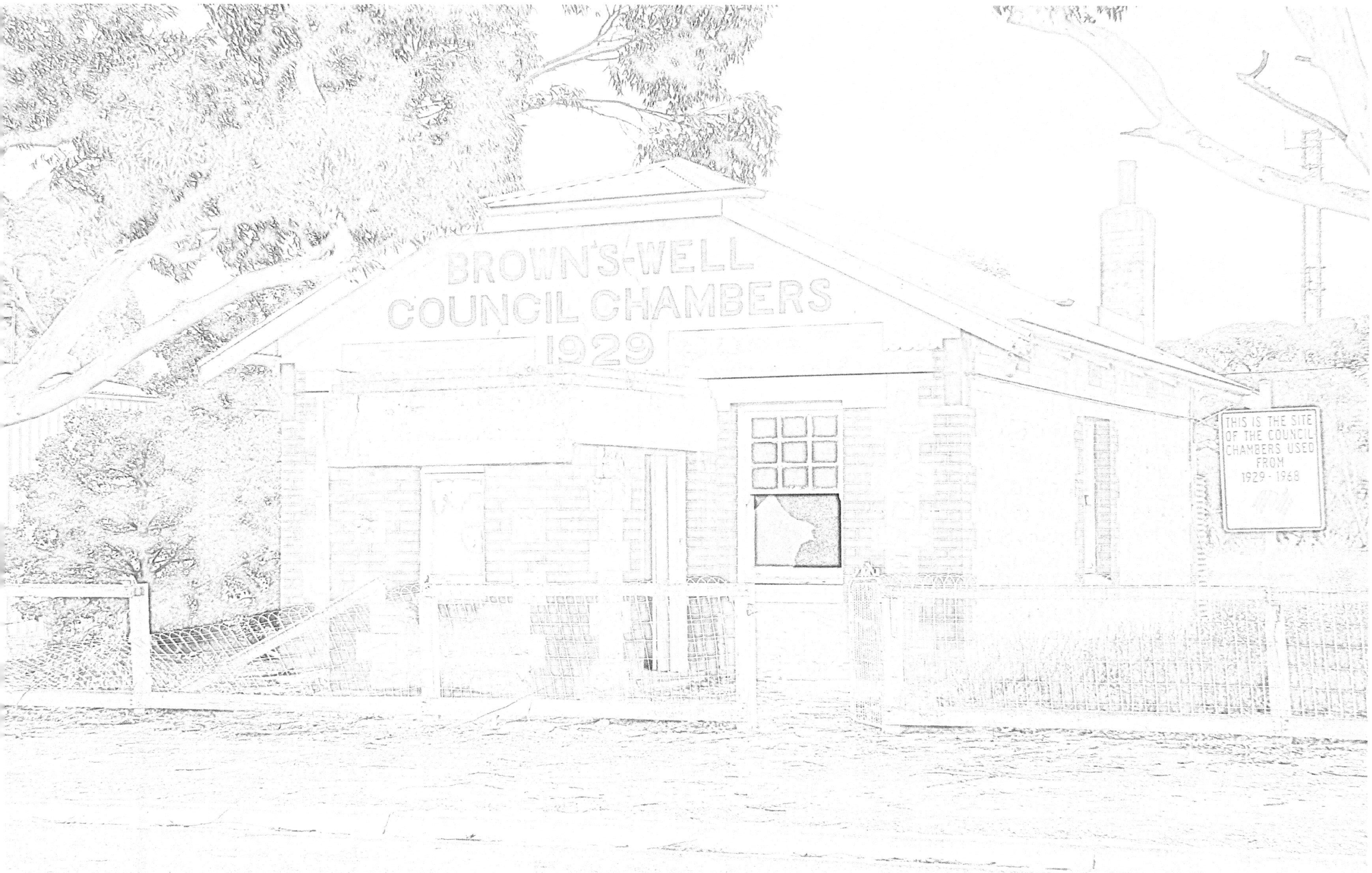
BROWN'S-WELL
COUNCIL CHAMBERS
1929
THIS IS THE SITE
OF THE COUNCIL
CHAMBERS USED
FROM
1929 - 1968

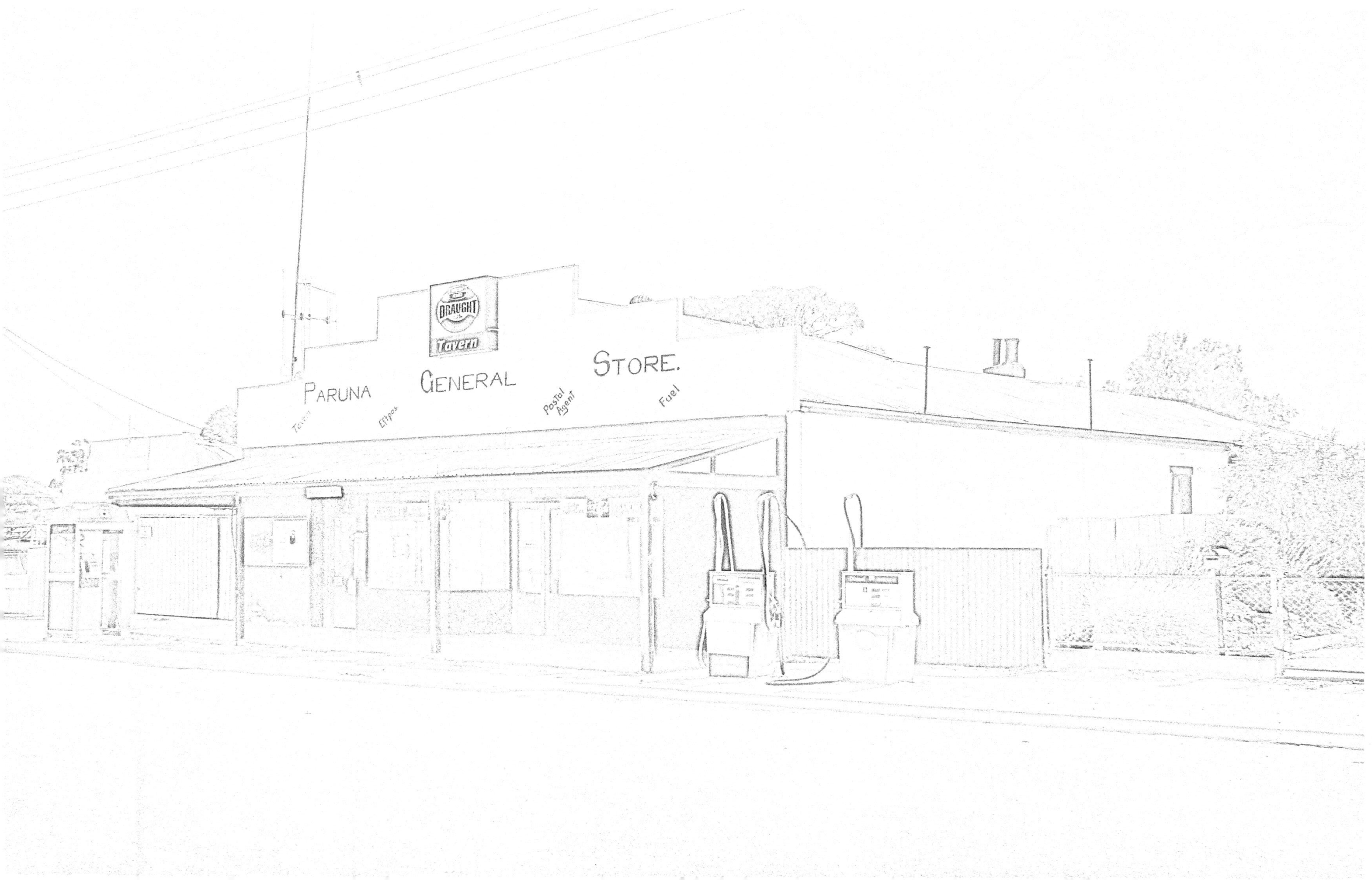
DRAUGHT
Tavern
PARUNA GENERAL STORE.
Eftpos
Postal Agent
Fuel

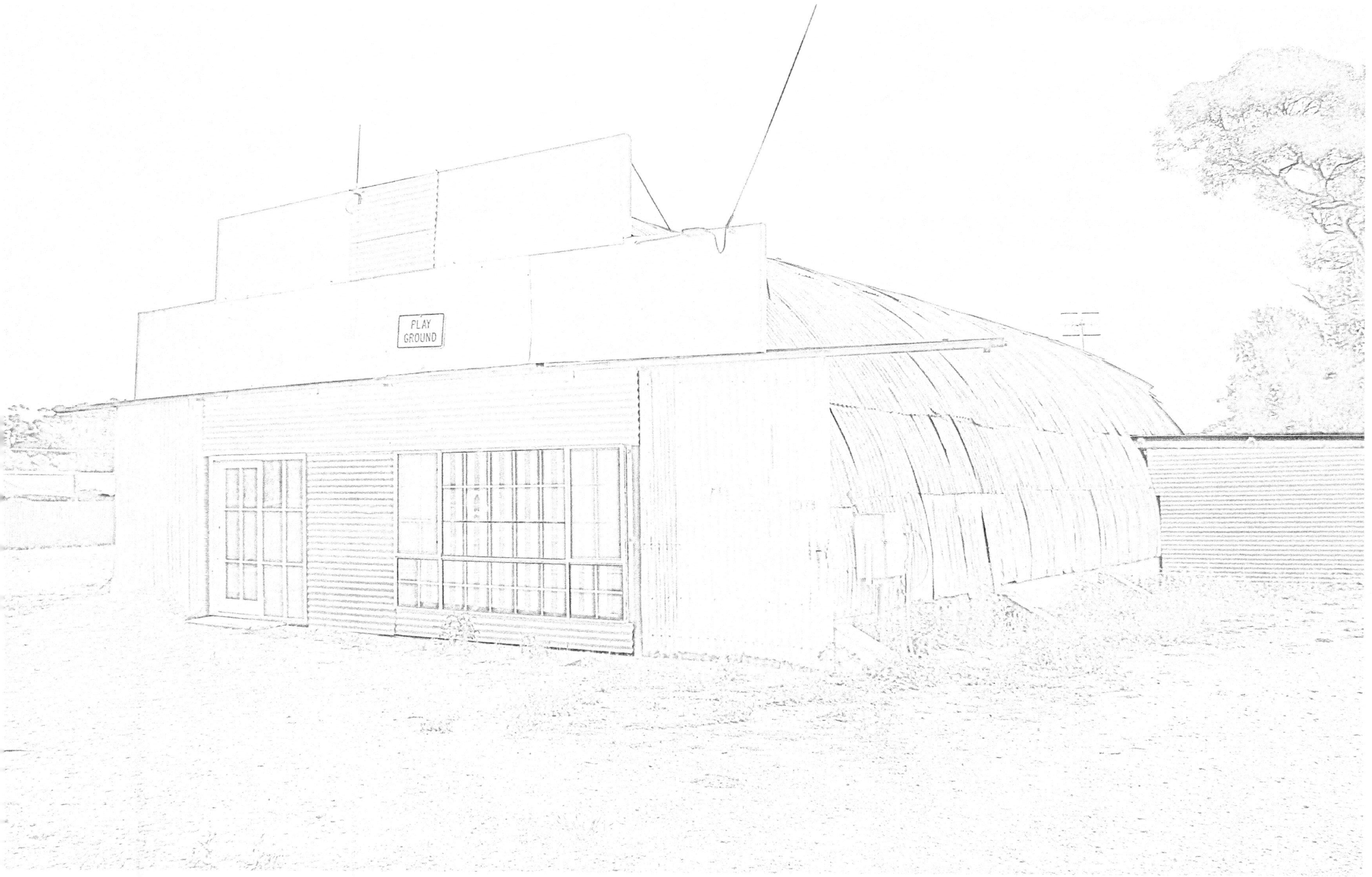
PLAY
GROUND

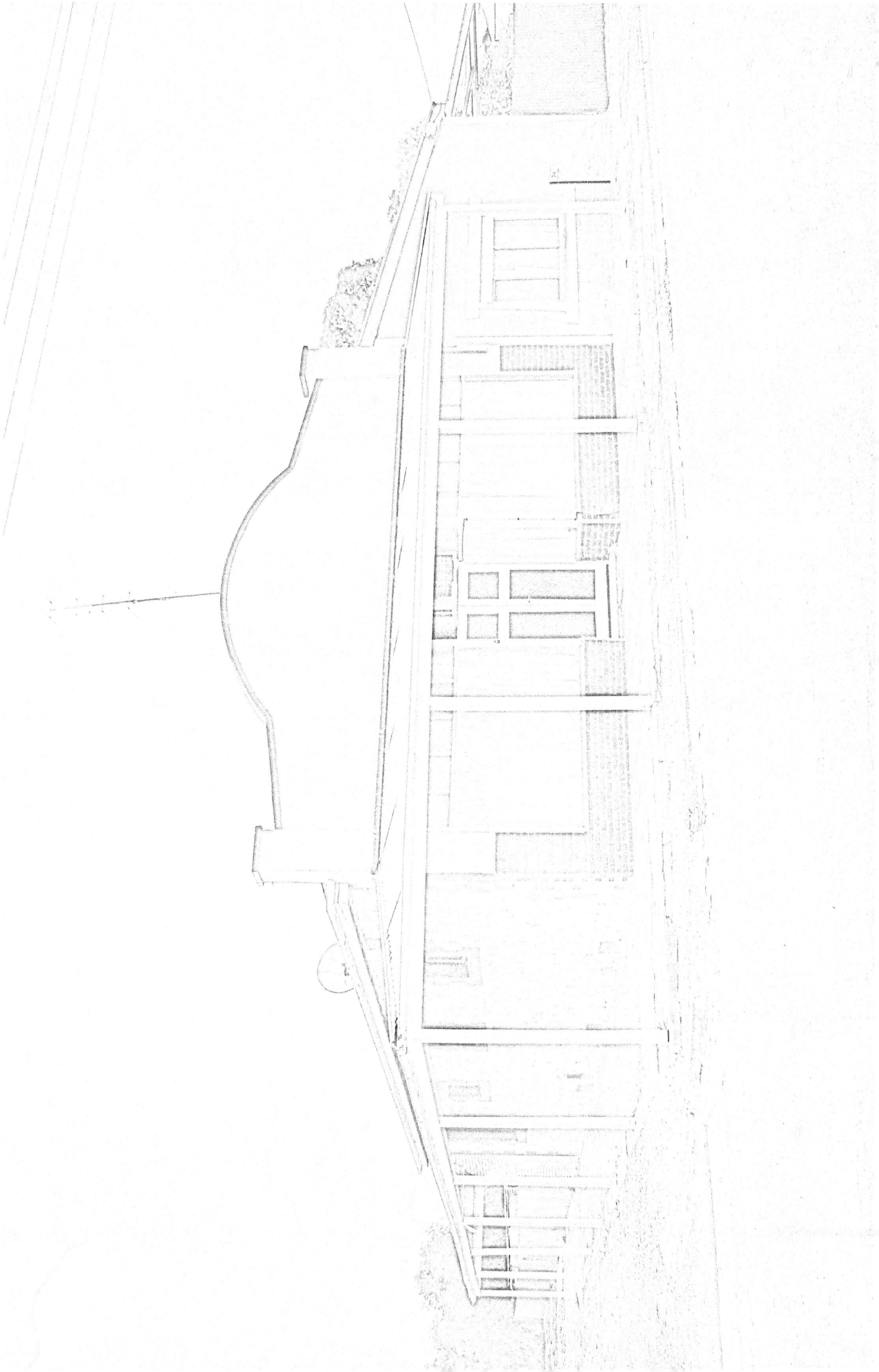

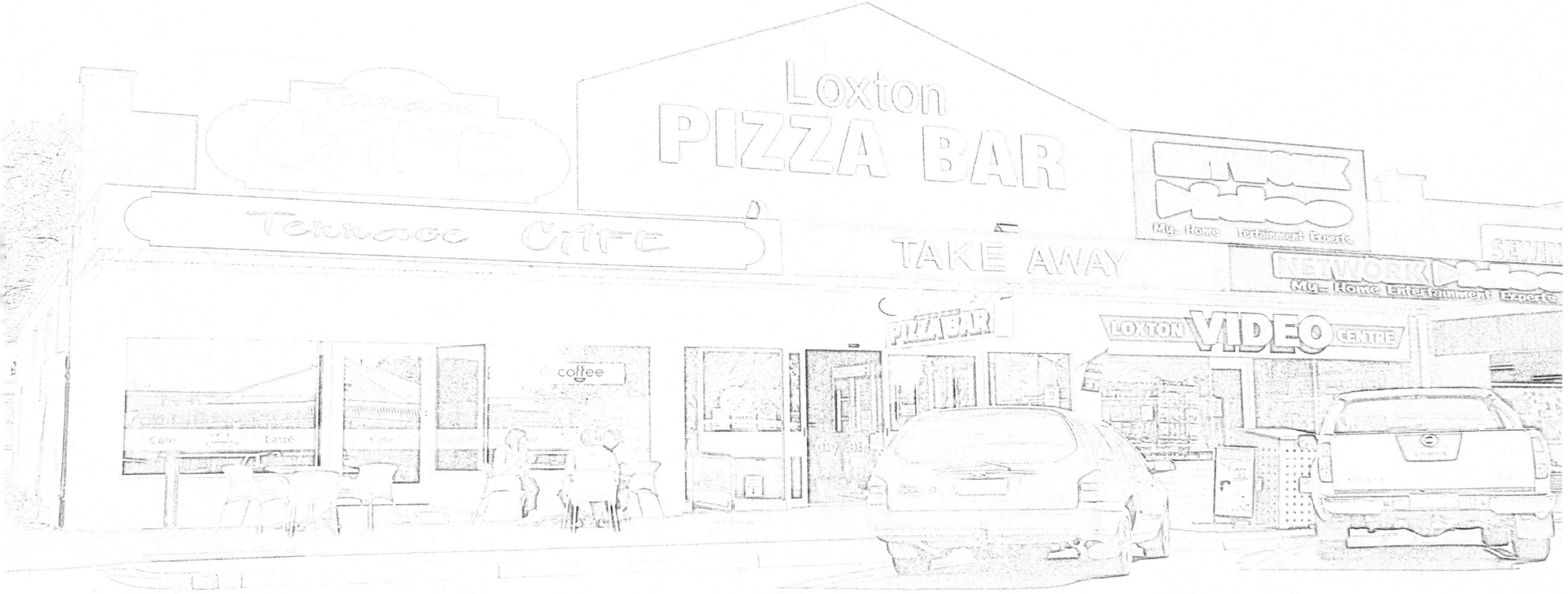

Loxton
PIZZA BAR
Terrace Cafe
TAKE AWAY
PIZZA BAR
LOXTON VIDEO CENTRE
NETWORK
My- Home Entertainment Experts
coffee

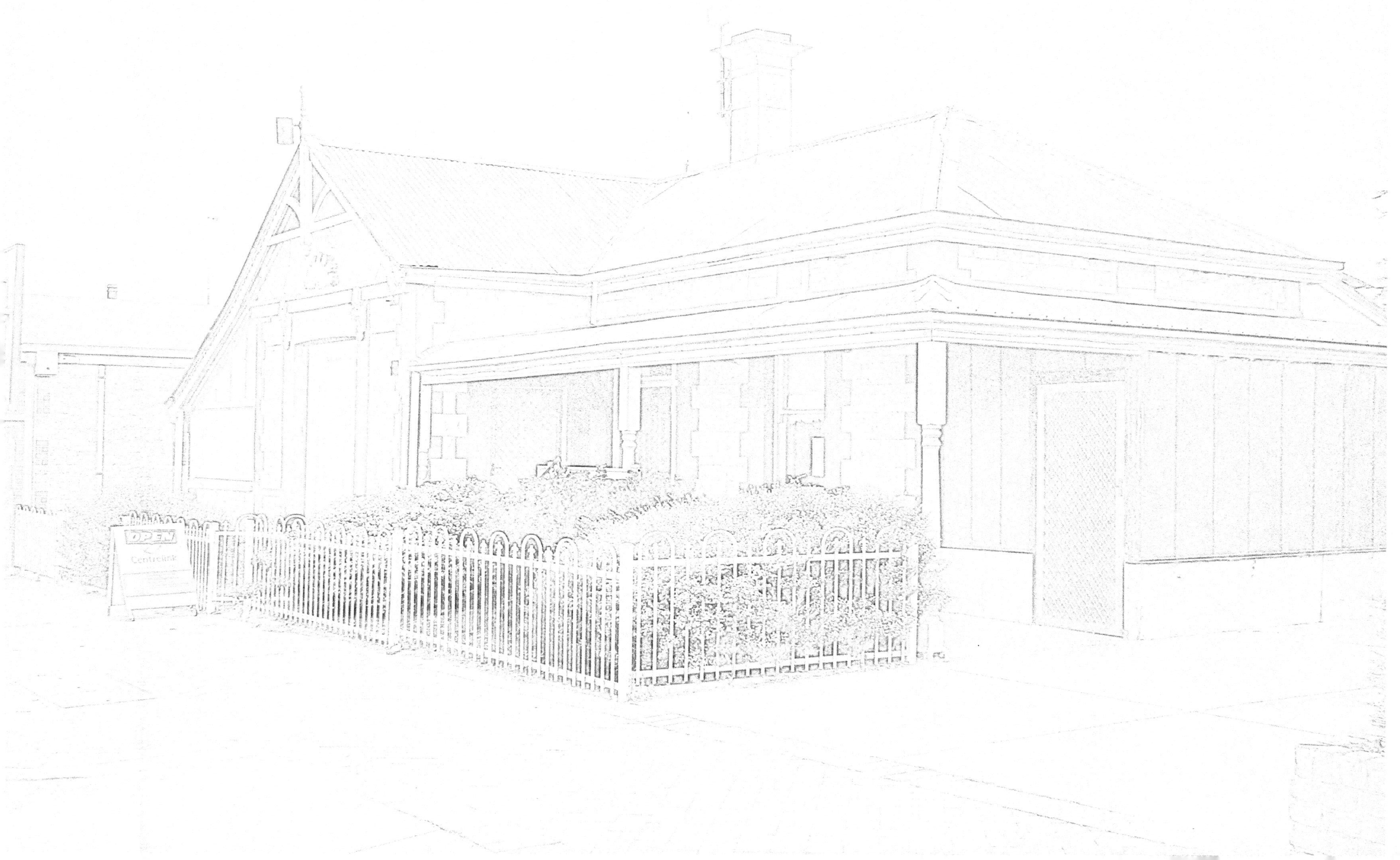
OPEN
Centrelink

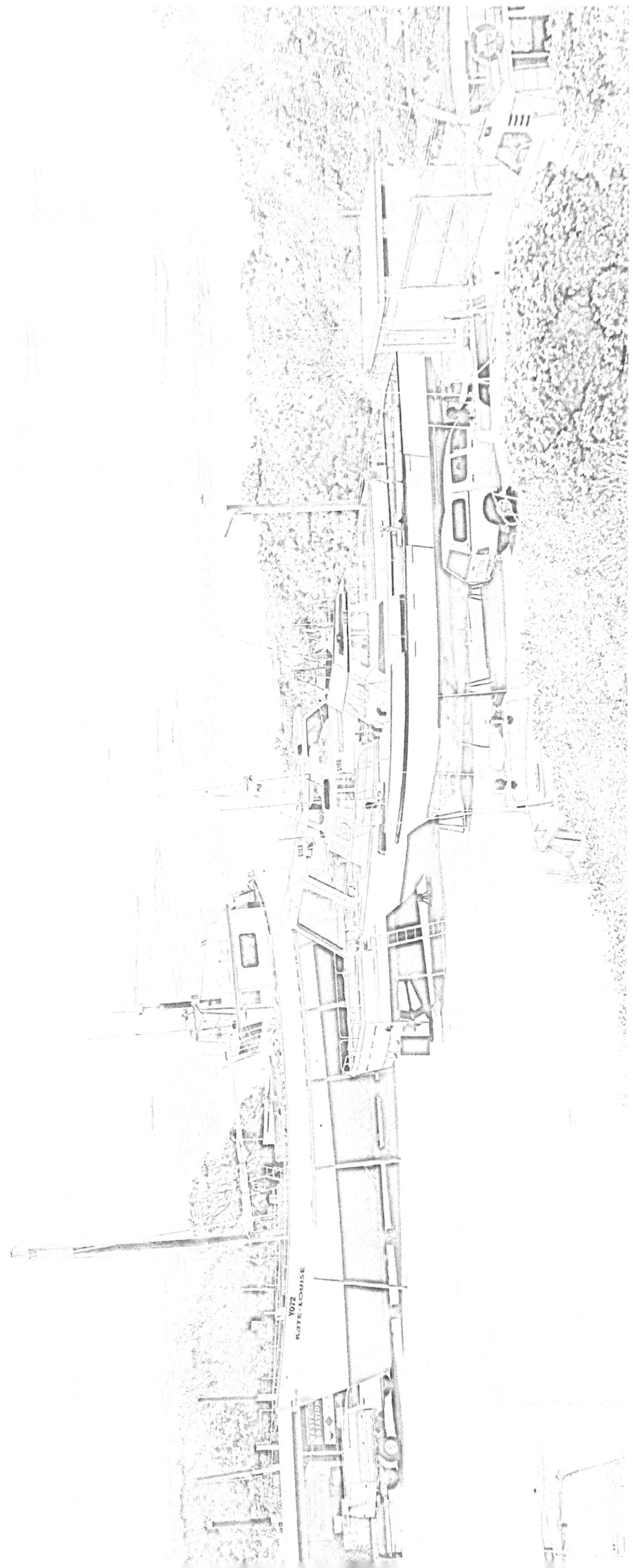
Y072

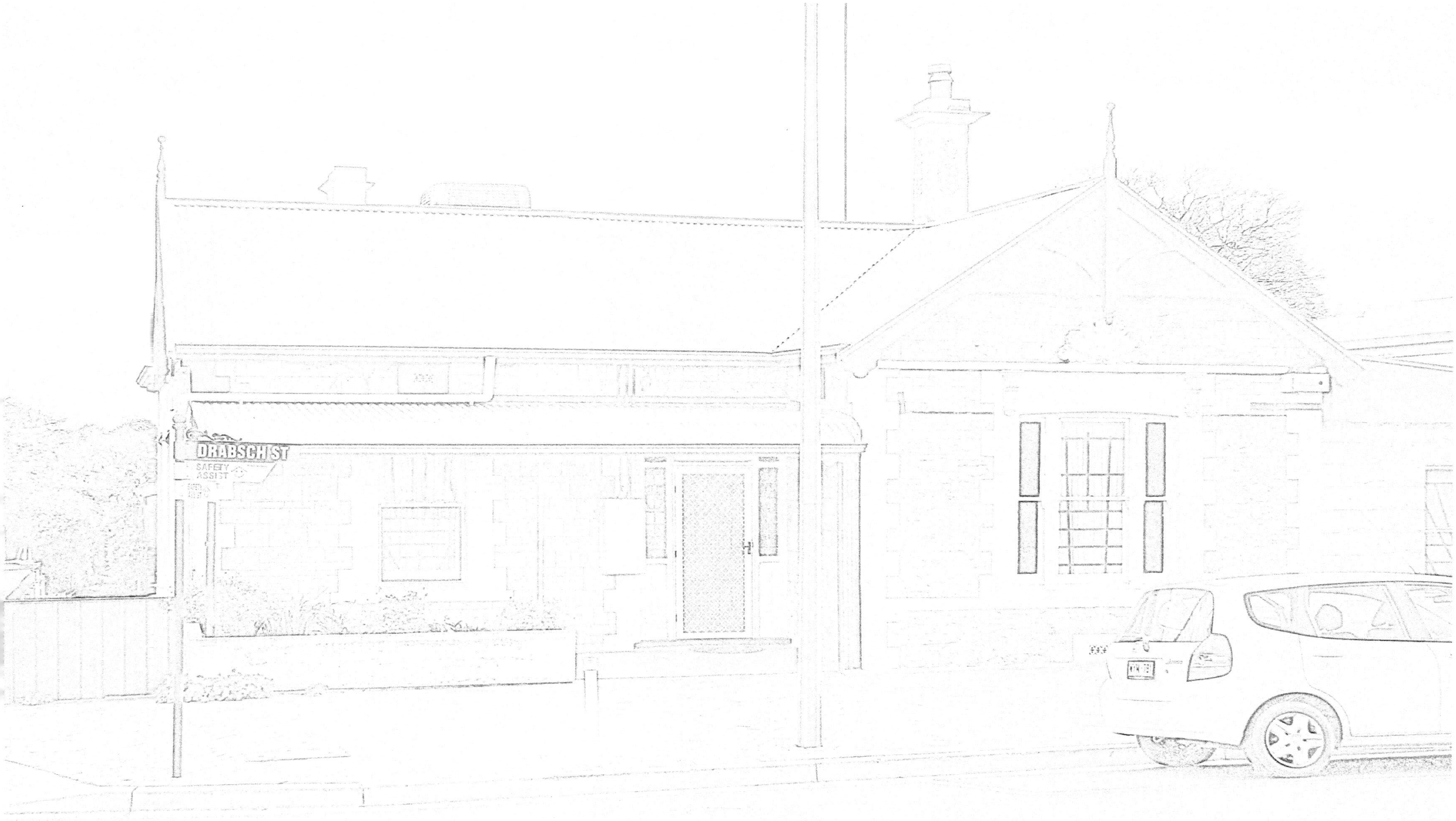
DRABSCH ST
SAFETY ASSIST

Loxton Soldiers Memorial
TALLY EX
Kodak Exp
FRAMING
EELIES BUS

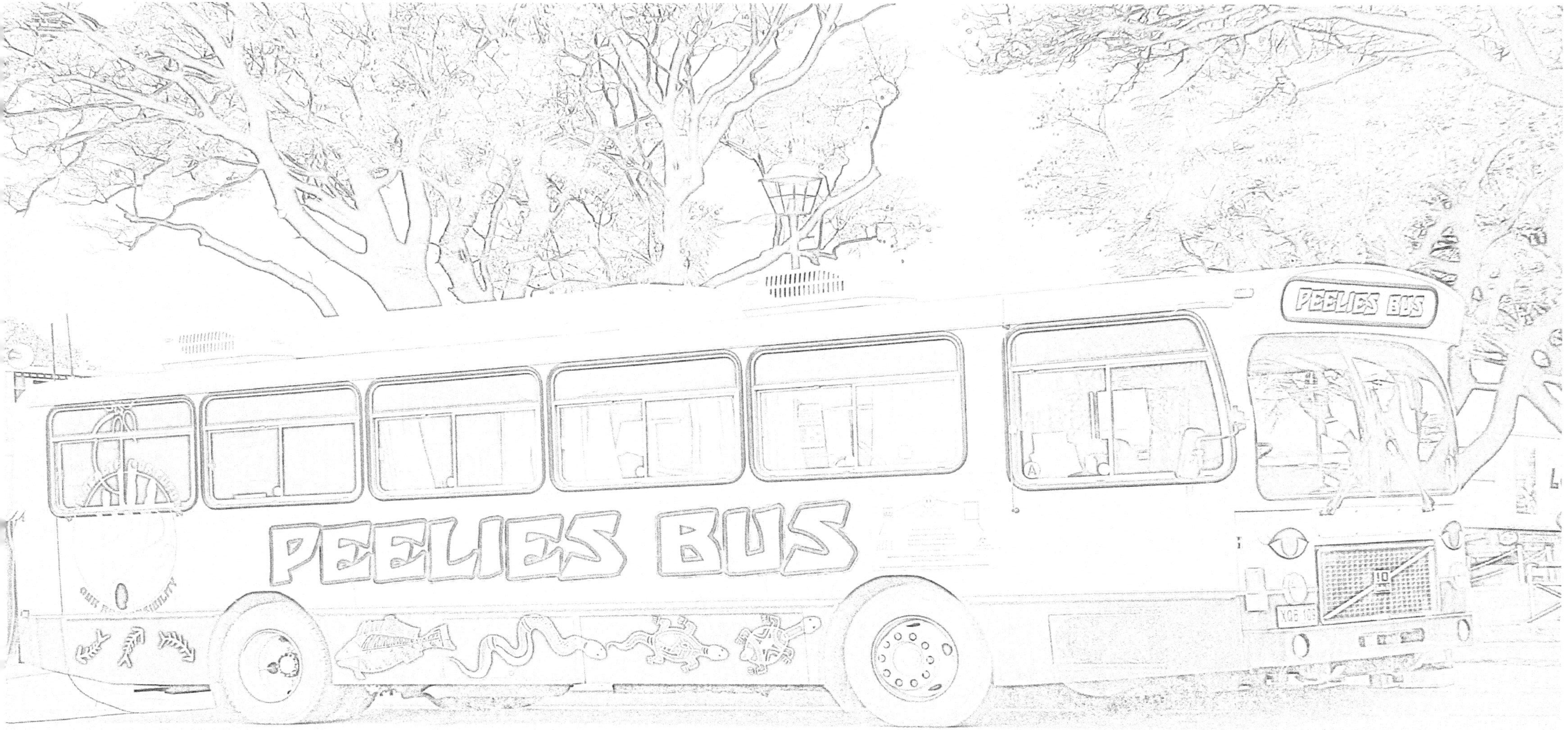
PEELIES BUS
PEELIES BUS

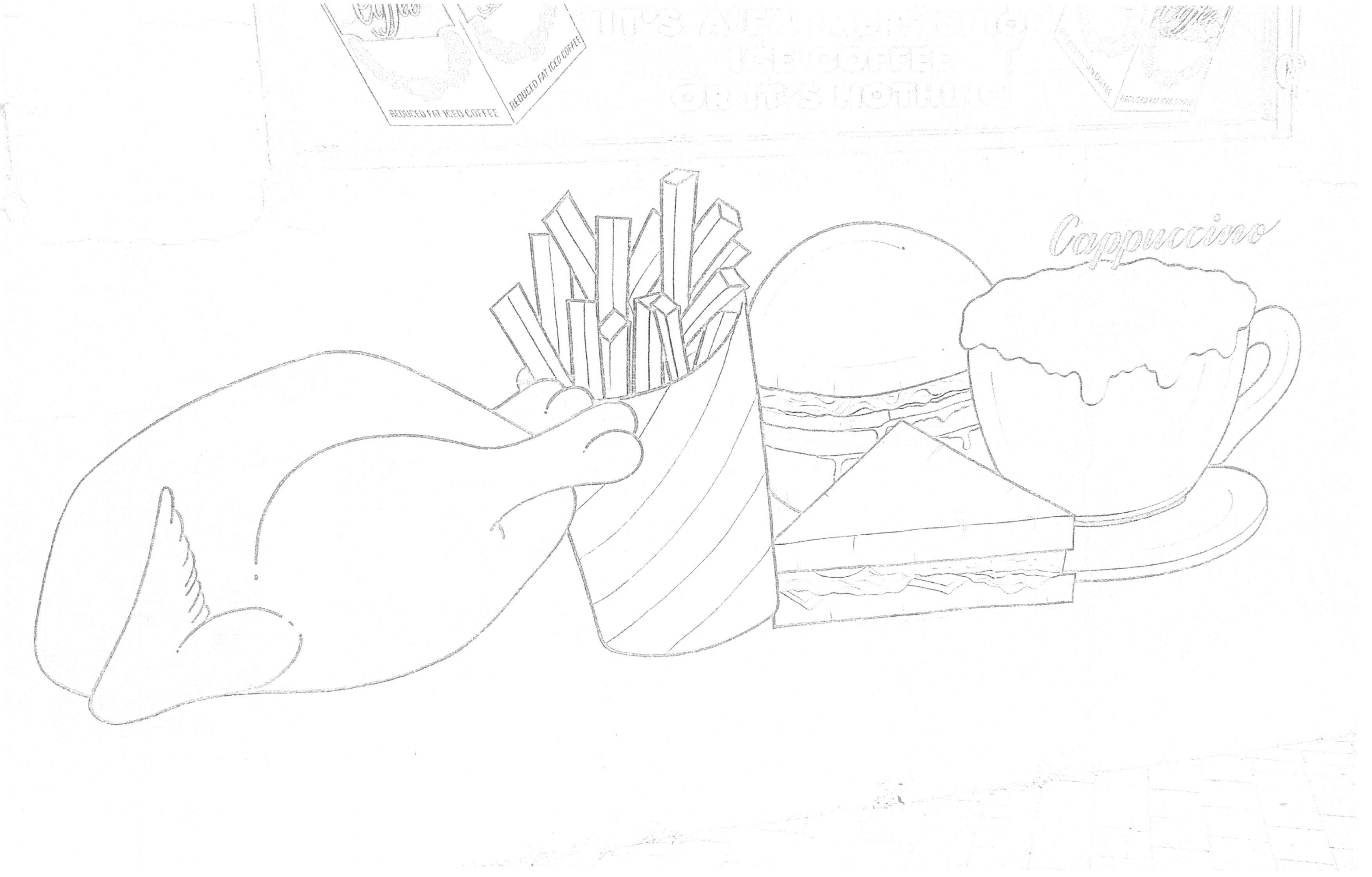
REDUCED FAT ICED COFFEE
REDUCED FAT ICED COFFEE
REDUCED FAT ICED COFFEE
Cappuccino

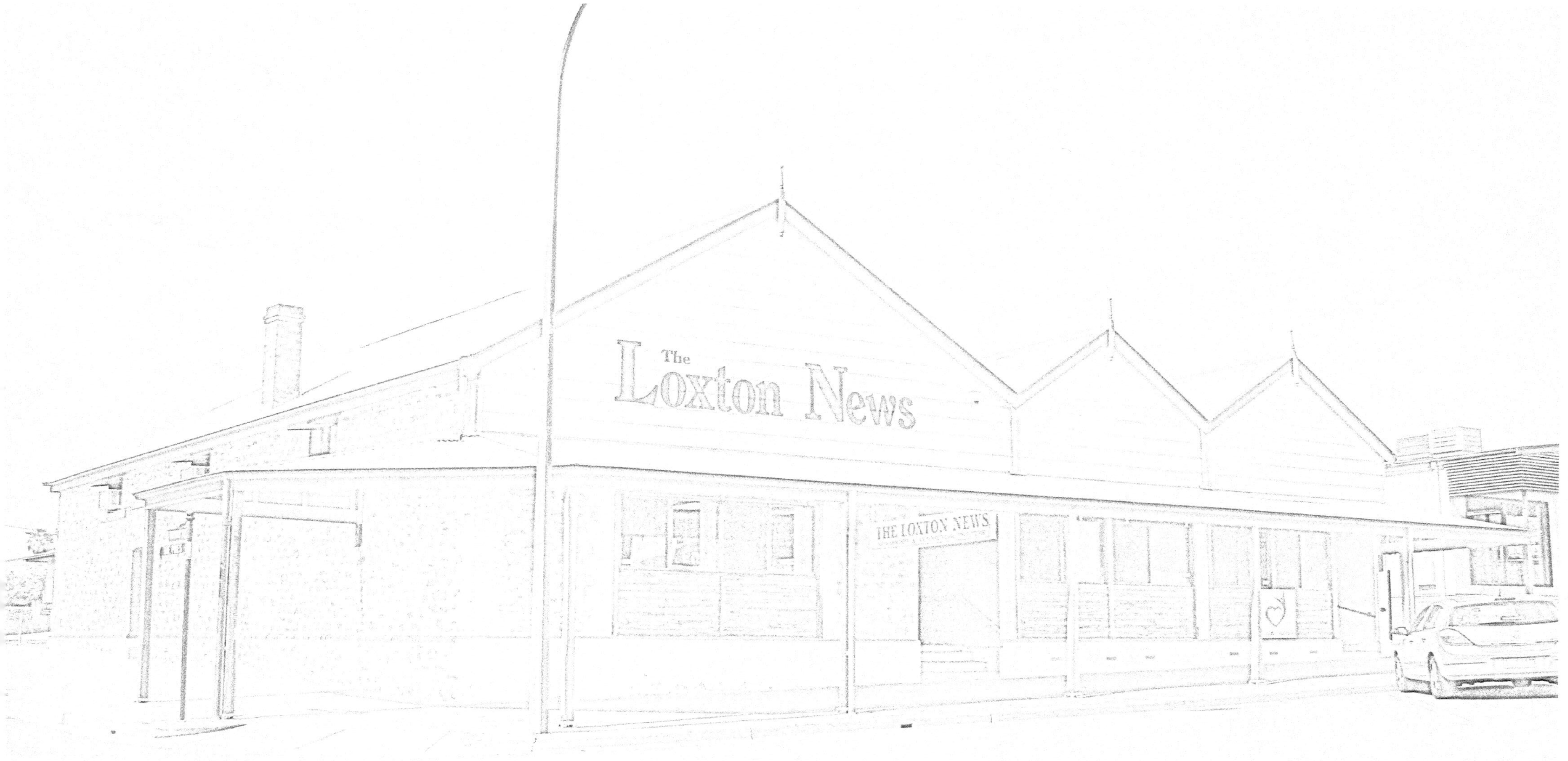
The Loxton News
THE LOXTON NEWS

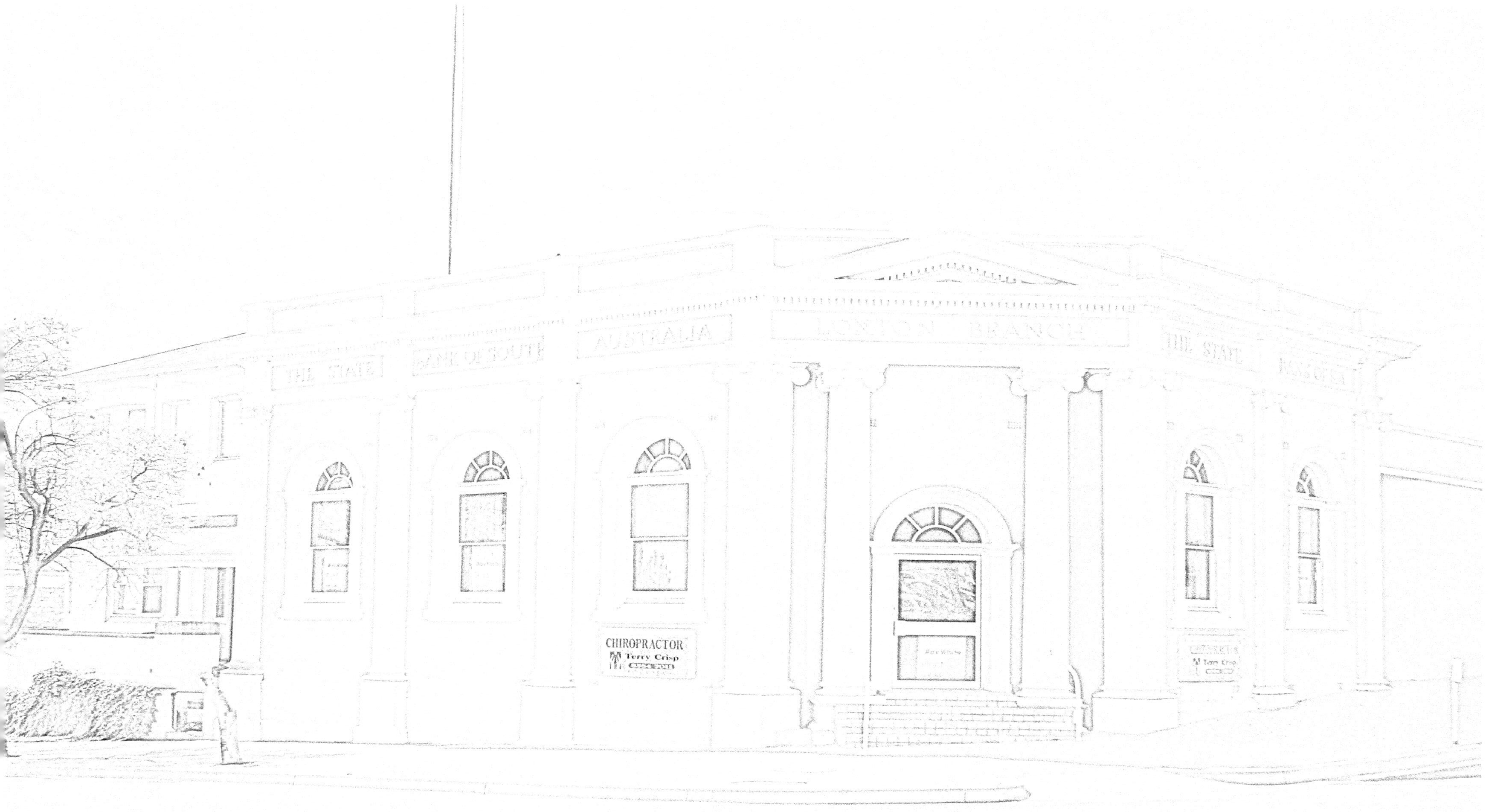
THE STATE BANK OF SOUTH AUSTRALIA
LOXTON BRANCH
THE STATE
CHIROPRACTOR
Terry Crisp

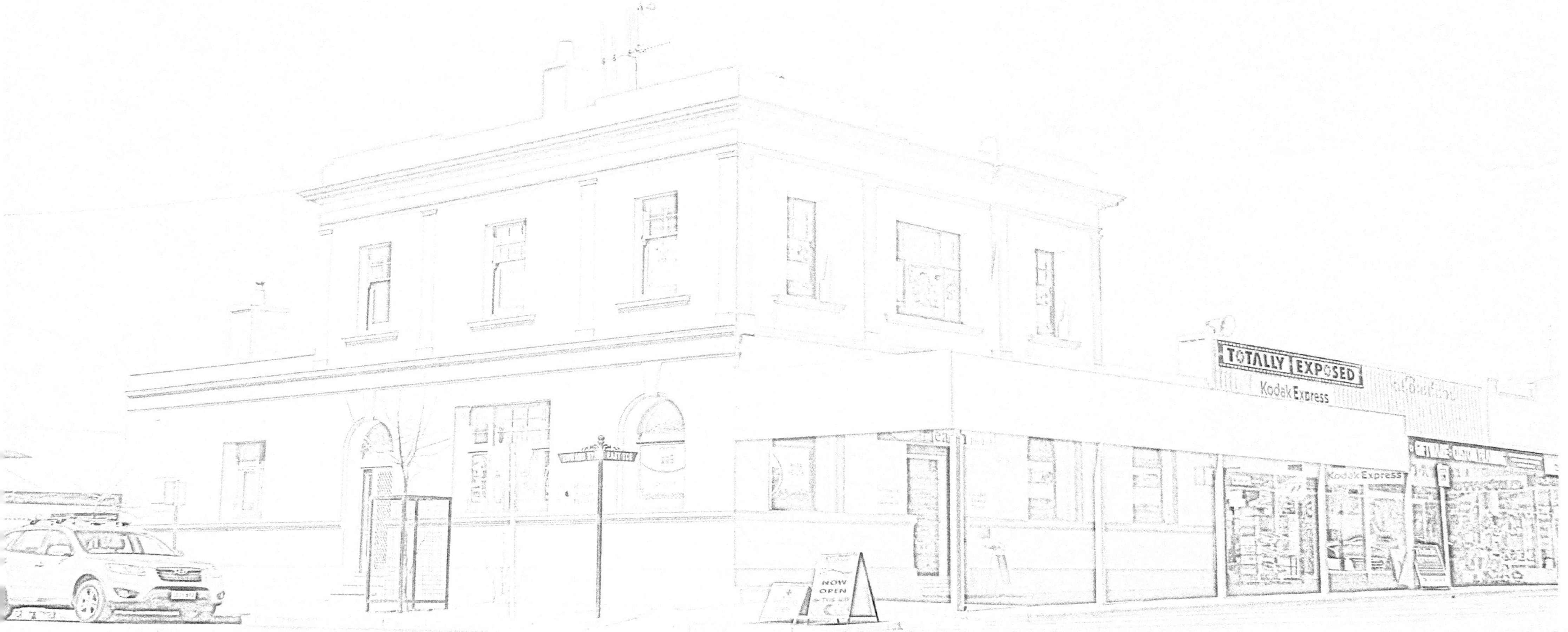
TOTALLY EXPOSED
Kodak Express
Kodak Express
NOW
OPEN

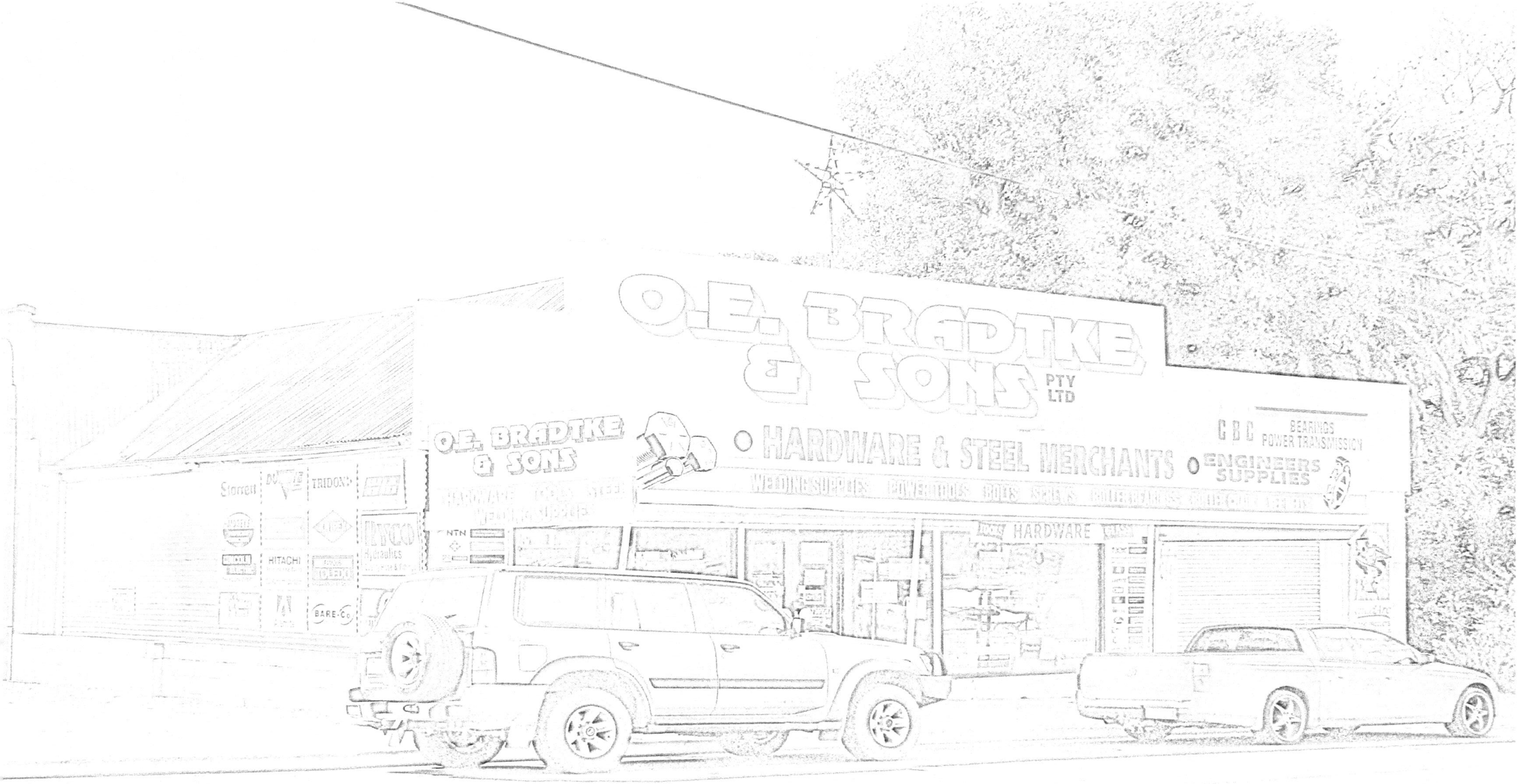
O.E. BRADTKE & SONS PTY LTD
HARDWARE & STEEL MERCHANTS
CBC BEARINGS POWER TRANSMISSION
ENGINEERS SUPPLIES
O.E. BRADTKE & SONS
HARDWARE
TRIDON
HITACHI
BARE-Co
NTN

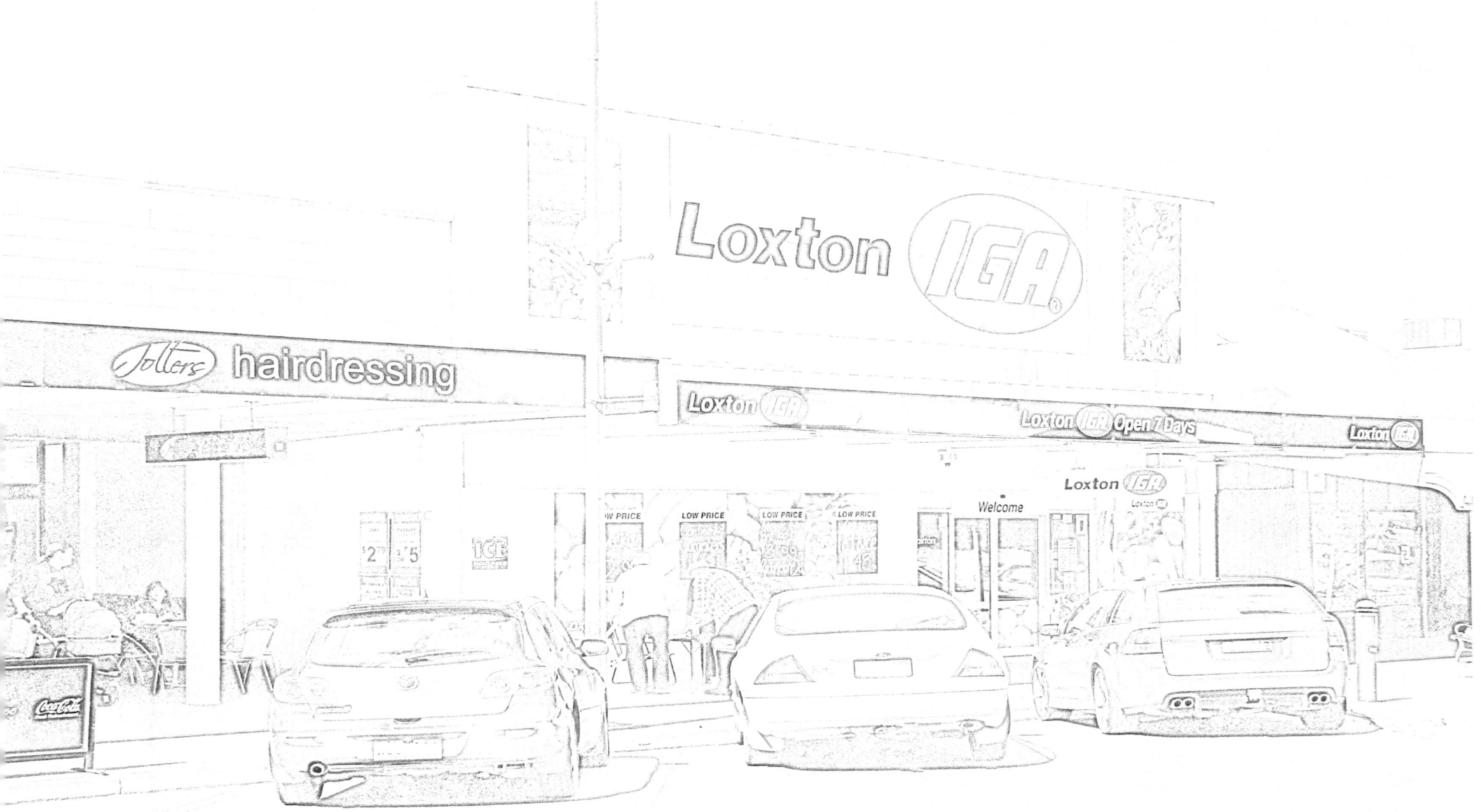
Loxton IGA
Jolters hairdressing
Loxton IGA
Loxton IGA Open 7 Days
Loxton IGA
Loxton IGA
Welcome
LOW PRICE
LOW PRICE
LOW PRICE
LOW PRICE
ICE
Coca-Cola

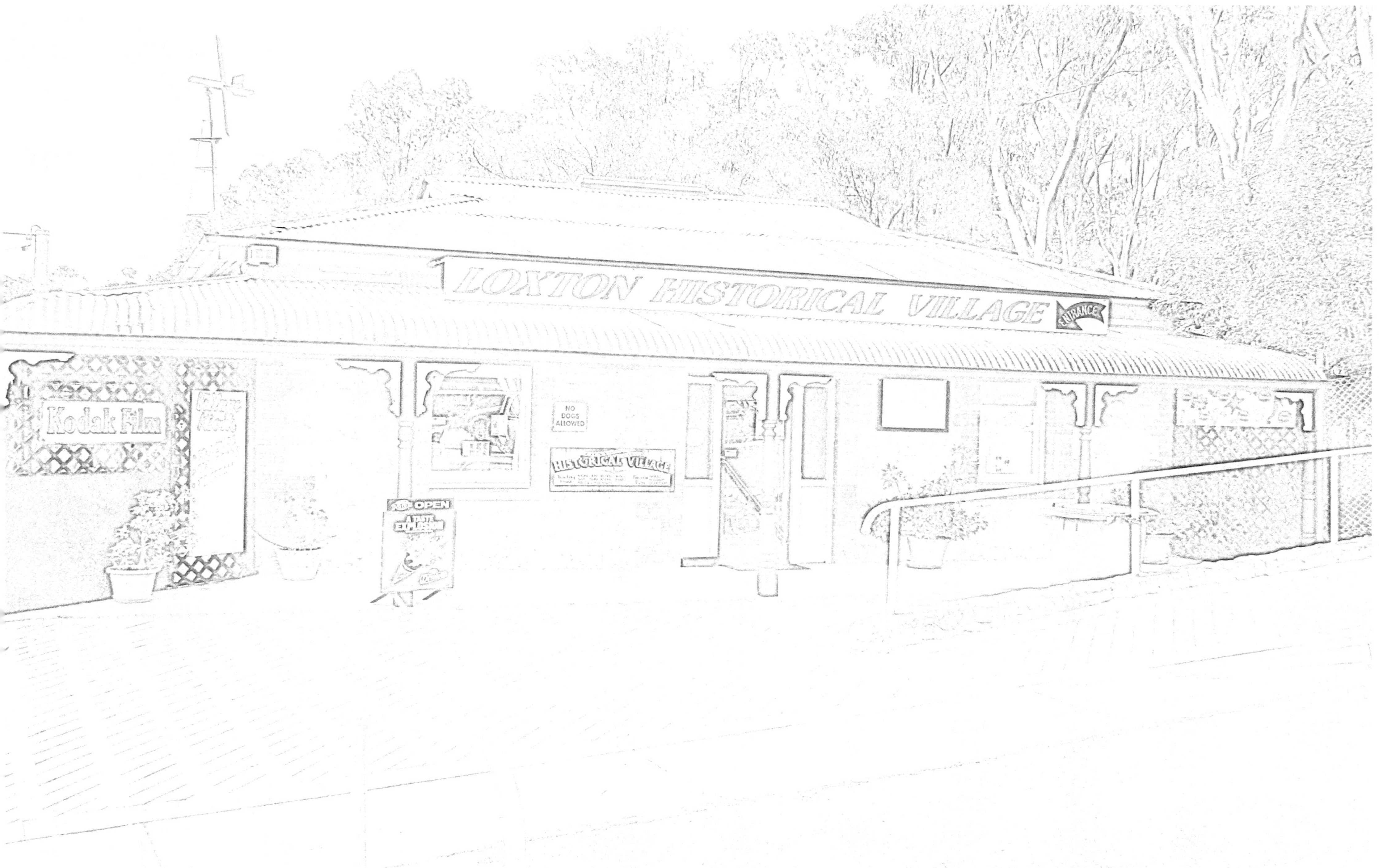

LOXTON HISTORICAL VILLAGE
ENTRANCE
Kodak Film
NO DOGS ALLOWED
HISTORICAL VILLAGE
OPEN
A TASTE EXPLOSION

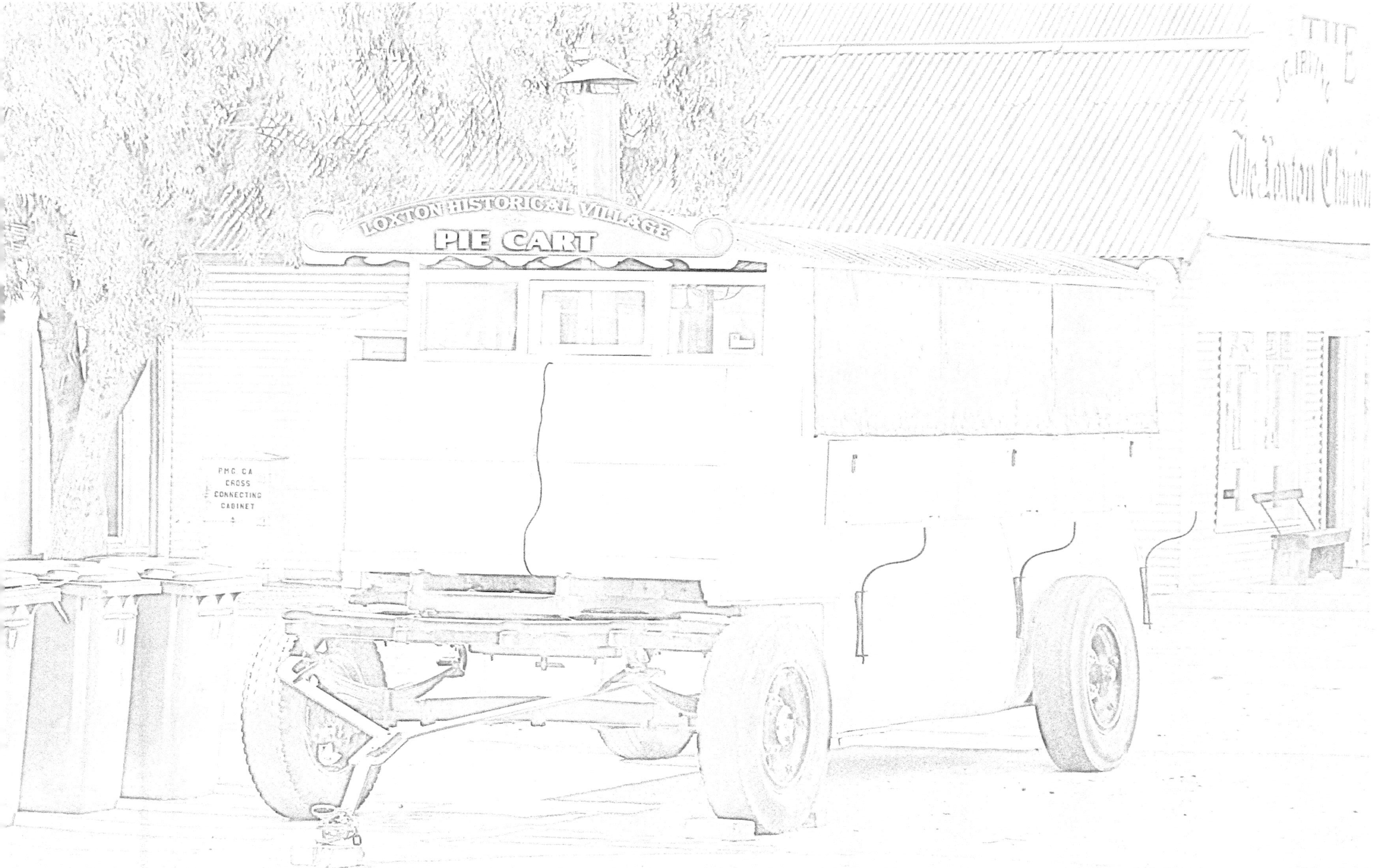
LOXTON HISTORICAL VILLAGE
PIE CART
PMG CA
CROSS
CONNECTING
CABINET

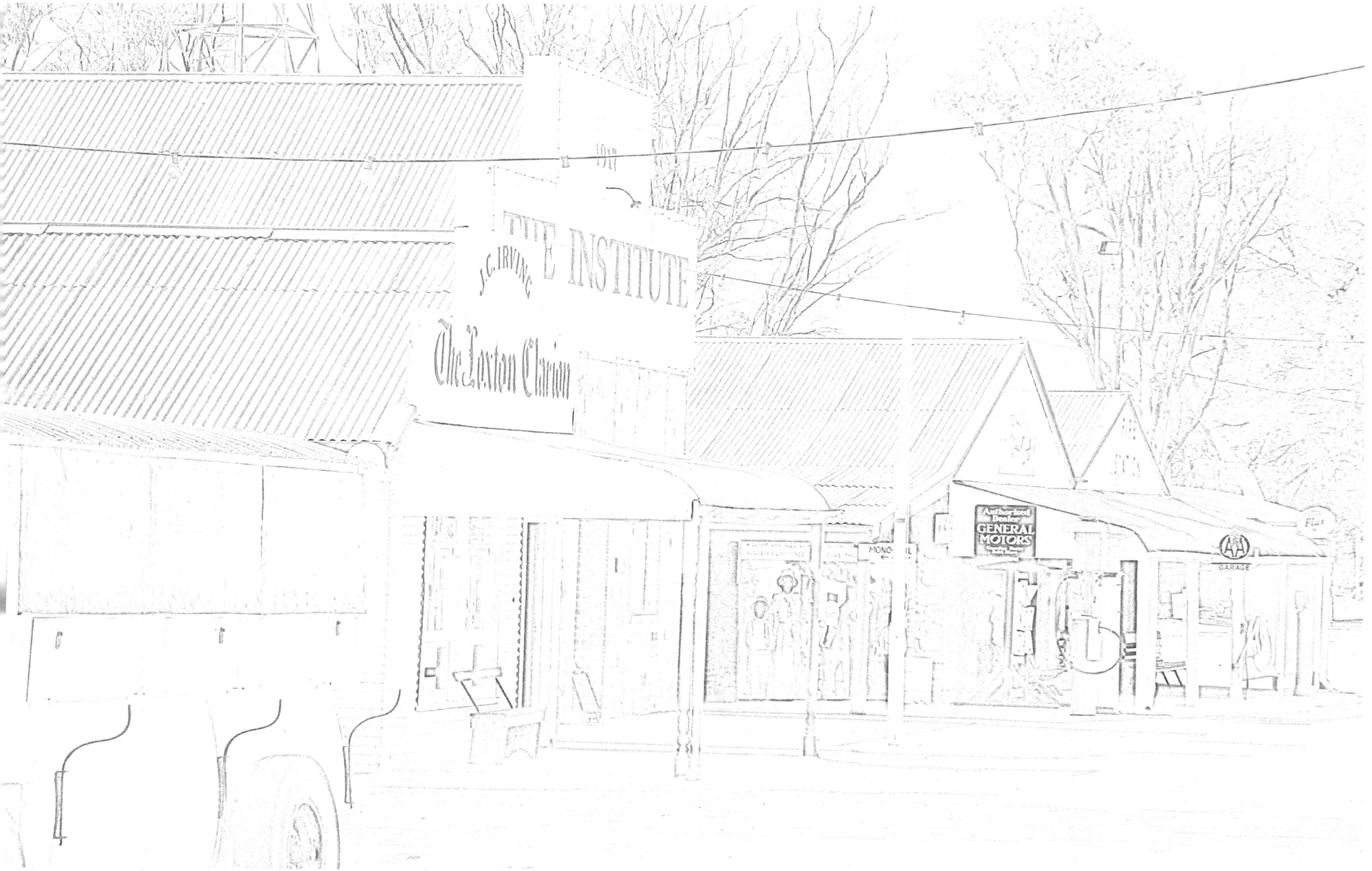
1917
THE INSTITUTE
J.C. IRVING
The Loxton Clarion
GENERAL MOTORS
MONO-
GARAGE

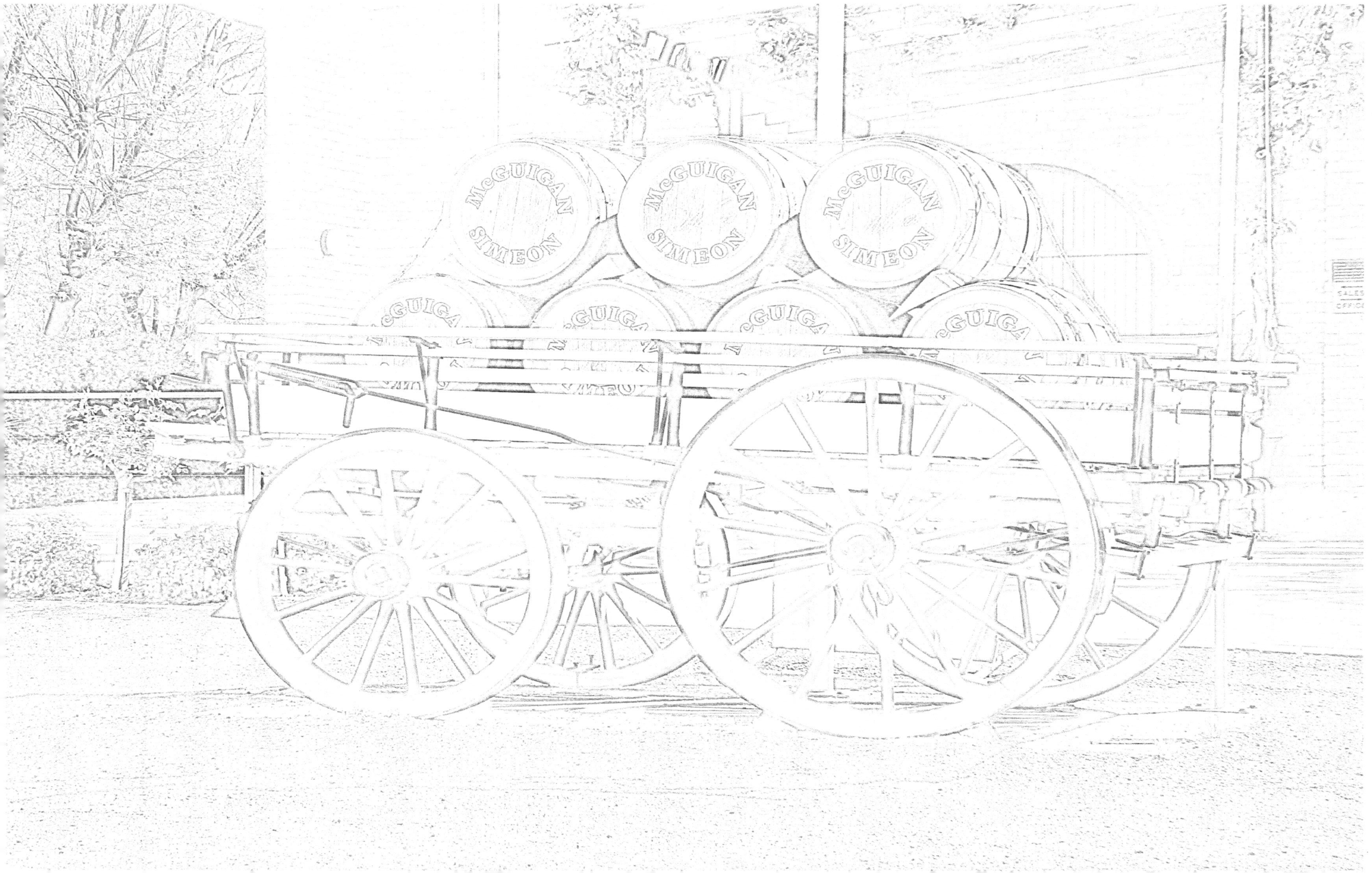
McGUIGAN
SIMEON

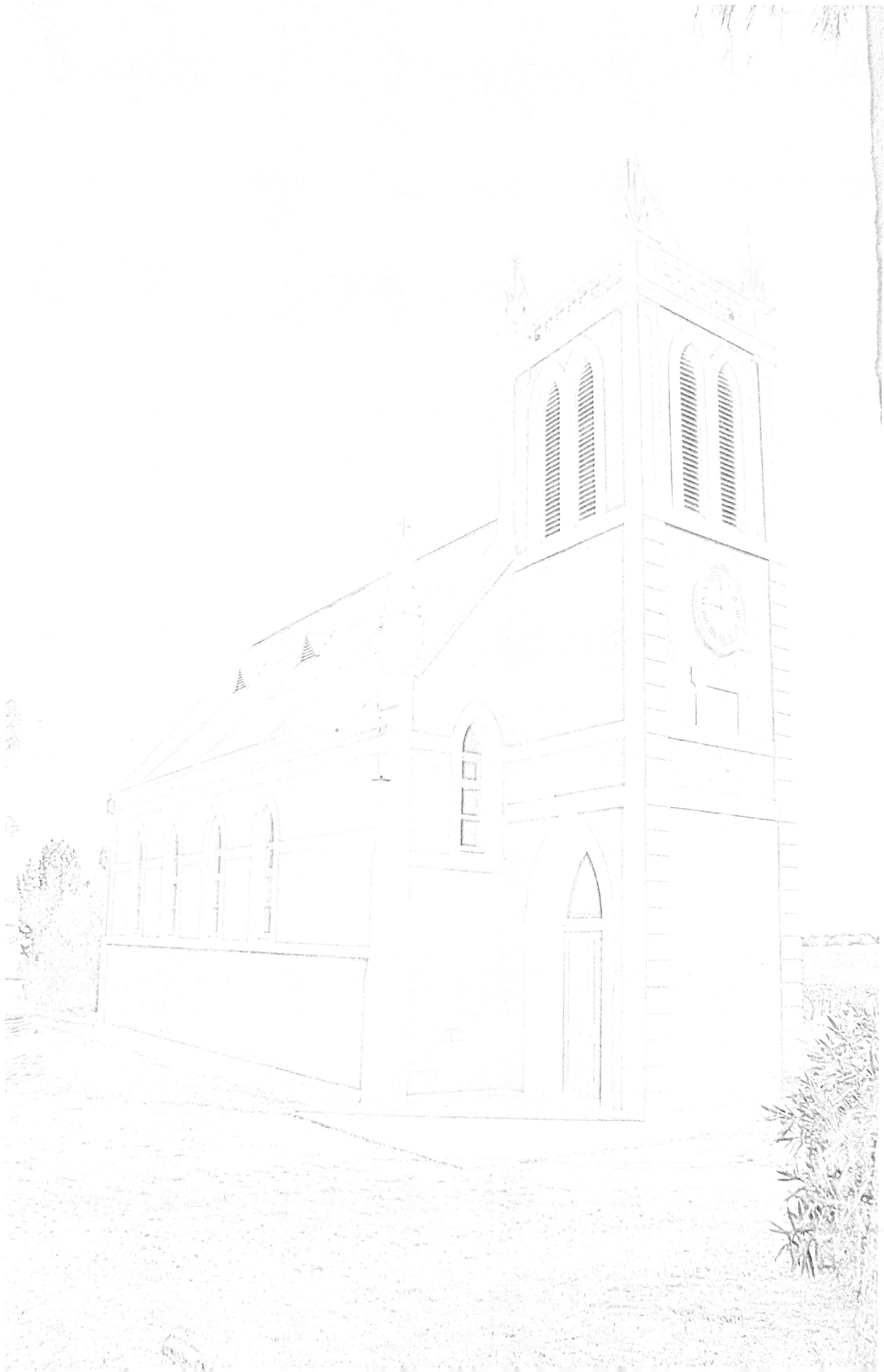

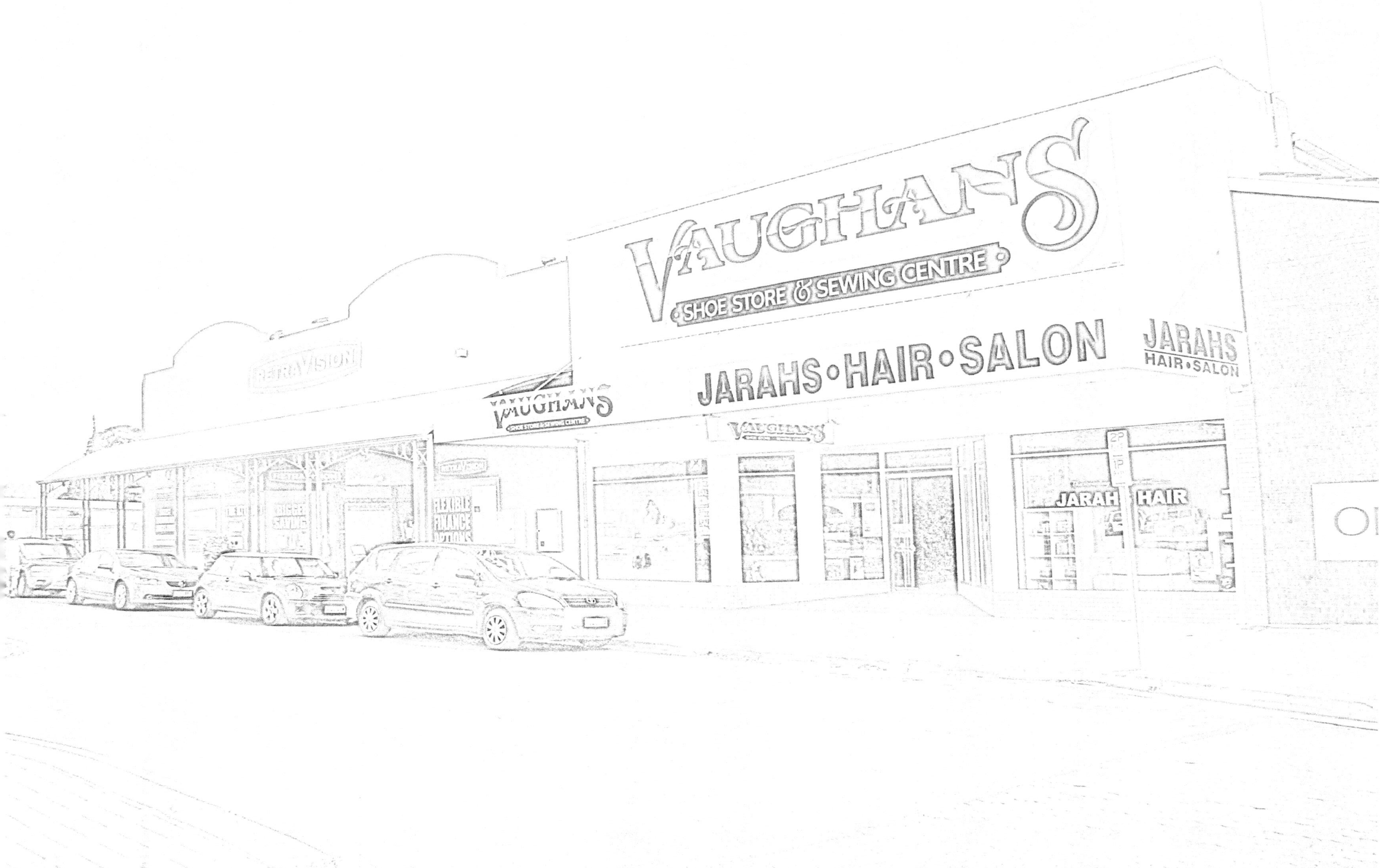
RETRAVISION
VAUGHANS
SHOE STORE & SEWING CENTRE
JARAHS • HAIR • SALON
JARAHS
HAIR • SALON
VAUGHANS
SHOE STORE & SEWING CENTRE
FLEXIBLE
FINANCE
OPTIONS
JARAH HAIR
2P
1P

www.ingramcontent.com/pod-product-compliance
Lightning Source LLC
Chambersburg PA
CBHW081057180526
45170CB00005B/1793